CUPBOARD LOVE

CUPBOARD LOVE

chin - chin !

Laura Lockington

Laura Lockington X

Book Guild Publishing

Sussex, England

First published in Great Britain in 2008 by
The Book Guild Ltd
Pavilion View
19 New Road
Brighton BN1 1UF

Typesetting in Perpetua by
Keyboard Services, Luton, Bedfordshire

Printed in Great Britain by
CPI Antony Rowe

A catalogue record for this book is available from
The British Library

ISBN 978 1 84624 280 9

To Damian Barr – *C.M.*

And to all the friends past and present that I've shared a meal with.
Especially, Mike 'Chutney' Moran
Jean-Yves 'Mayonnaise' Aubin
Sue 'Rib Eye' Sinclair
Megan 'Balsamic' Verilly
Carol 'Hot Milk on the Side' Biss
Simon 'Bagelman' Lock
Kerry 'Growler' Herbert
Jaq 'Kalamata Olives' Aris
Alice 'Choccy' Taylor
Kate 'Porridge and Cream' Hanbury
Paul 'Broadbean' Ostrer
Andrew 'Dim Sum' Kay
and David 'Red Only' Mitchell

Contents

Introduction

I don't care what anyone says. Losing your virginity does not make you an adult. Nor does getting your first credit card. Or buying your first house. Or making a will. Cooking your first Christmas lunch: that's about as grown up as it gets.

My life has been marked by the meals I've had. My first day at school is all but forgotten, but I remember the lovingly cooked perfect soft boiled egg with toasted soldiers. I couldn't with any certainty describe my first wedding dress or the shoes I wore on that ill-fated honeymoon, but I could tell you what I had for dinner. I've already planned my funeral menu (lucky guests will offset their grief with cold lobster, Jean-Yves's mayonnaise and the walnut bread from that little baker round the corner).

It's time to admit; I have an unhealthy interest in food. Not just my food. But your food. His food, her food, their food. In restaurants I peer at other people's plates. In supermarkets I forensically examine other people's trolleys. It's not that I want what they have, I just want to know what they're having. I am a food stalker.

If you're as bored or curious (some might say nosey) as I am don't bother browsing the bookshelves or raiding the medicine cabinet – try reading the fridge. Knowing what someone reads for amusement or takes for indigestion is nowhere as revealing as knowing what they have for breakfast. Out of date yoghurt? A student that hasn't learnt how to shop (or cook). A tupperware box of homemade granola? A diet conscious fool. Champagne, Loch Fyne kippers and home made marmalade? Marry them.

Food is as revealing as money sex or religion. More so. And it's revealed more often – with every meal or snack. How often do we hear that someone can't eat fish? Or that they crave chocolate, have a hatred of sprouts and or are forbidden coffee? We hear all about all their dietary preferences but never their true bank balance. As for sex, well, we only hear what they want us to hear.

Our relationship with food determines our relationships with others. Some people swear you can predict the performance of a potential lover simply by watching him dance. I'd rather watch him eat a pomegranate. Is he picking the ruby seeds out one by one or tearing it apart with his hands? Is he prissy about getting the crimson juice on his shirt or is he happily wiping his mouth with the back of his hand? Does the bitter yellow pith bother him or is he attacking it with gusto? I think we all know which is right.

I once broke up with a partner between courses. We'd been together for five years. After the lamb I left the room to get the summer fruit pudding. He left me while I was in the kitchen. And there was clotted cream, too.

What did *your* mother make for you when *you* were ill? When my first husband had the flu he begged me to make him a quite revolting lunch involving coley – that very grey fish old ladies buy for their cats – and tinned tomato soup.

Perhaps equally revolting to you is my belief in the healing properties of mashed banana.

Our reaction to food is not rational. What we choose to eat depends on our past and personal experiences. The food we choose tells us very clearly who we choose to be and to be with. More than religion, football teams or daily newspapers. More than anything.

What we eat is as telling as what we wear. Food has fashions. Just as telling as the woman who wears a mini skirt and outlines her eyes in kohl decades after it has been *au courant*, is the man who insists on having his steak burnt beyond recognition à la 1960s. I realise now that my early childhood was guided by Edwardian mores. This was partly because my grandmother, born in 1861, ruled the roost. And partly because my parents, to whom I appeared as a surprise late in life, were the tail end of her generation. They had both lived and worked through World War II. Even now, in a time of relative excess, they had reverted to her style of eating. The food and lifestyle revolution caused by Elizabeth David and Terence Conran did not hit our household till quite late.

Our food habits and feelings are so deeply ingrained that, even if we stopped and questioned them, we simply wouldn't get an answer. You either like whelks or you don't. I once saw a close friend of mine prepare a leg of lamb for roasting. She laboriously cut off the knuckle bone and slipped it beside the joint. I asked her why she did that. Because my mother did, was her reply. She phoned her mother to ask her why she had. *She* said that *her* mother always had. Grandma was duly called and cackled with laughter. 'You fools! I did it because my roasting tray was too small for the joint!' Makes you wonder, doesn't it?

So I have decided to delve back and try to discover how and why I eat as I do. It may be as foolish as chips without salt or gin without tonic. But I have to know. What is it that makes me cook for the people I love? Is it something that we all do? Is food fuel for living or loving? Live to eat or eat to live? Do I need to unchain myself from the stove? Kitchen or bedroom? Can you have both (without a house fire or large laundry bills)?

Love and food. It's all in there somewhere.

Chapter 1

Grandmothers:
Putting the Fun in Funeral

Ham Cooked in Cider

Even if your butcher assures you that it doesn't need soaking, it probably does. Place in cold water and leave overnight or for at least five hours.

2kg 'green' gammon
1 large bottle cloudy cider
stick of celery
1 carrot
1 onion
8 peppercorns
2 bayleaves
(For the glaze – dark sugar, English mustard
powder, cloves)

Place the ham in the largest pan you have, pour over the cider, and pop the onion, carrot, celery, bayleaves and peppercorns in. If the cider doesn't cover the meat, top it

1

up with water. Bring to the boil and then simmer for two and a half hours. Allow to cool or you will burn your fingers horribly. Take the rind off, and score the fat in criss crosses with a sharp knife. Rub with a handful of mustard powder and sugar. Stud with cloves and then place in hot oven till the outside is as brown as you would wish – about twenty minutes to half an hour.

Delicious. I promise you will never buy pre-packed ham ever again.

The two grandmothers were formidable in their separate ways.

Grace Helen had been a beauty and a card sharp. A cruel series of strokes kept her bedridden in my childhood home in Kent: a regal figure swathed in black silk shawls and heavy amber necklaces, a silver topped ebony cane kept by the bedside which was tapped imperiously when anything was wanted. Her once chestnut hair, now white, she is a refuge from anything that needs to be avoided. Whole days are spent in the comfort of her heavily blanketed bed playing snap or shops, wrapping up small china objects from her highly polished wooden cabinet in newspaper and then bartering with one another over the price. The silky strips of ribbon that hemmed the purple wool of her bedclothes are rubbed away to a silvery sheen by my fingers. She belongs to the days of corsets, tortoiseshell hairpins and lace handkerchiefs drenched in eau de cologne. Low slung elegant cars had driven her down the corniche to 'Monte'. She has a sharp tongue and a kind heart.

When an optician made a house call to check her failing

sight she was convinced he'd left the room and whispered in a piercing hiss to my mother: 'Joan, thank goodness that dreadful man has left, he *smells*. I'm sure he wets himself!' He hasn't left. My mother covers her confusion in a torrent of words.

A plate of fruit with a silver and mother of pearl fruit knife is always on her bedside table. Just the names of the apples were enough to make you think she was reciting a litany. Pearmain, Beauty of Bath, Bloody Butcher (causing hysterical giggles from me, because it was so rude), Crimson King (the words reversed years later to become the name of a rock band that I played very loudly in my bedroom whilst dousing myself in patchouli oil), Foxwhelp, Captain Kidd, Cornish Honeypin, Court Royal, Doll's Eye, Gloria Mundi, James Grieve and many others that can probably only be found now at Kew Gardens. If at all.

Her endless supply of fruit is delivered, along with all other staples to the house. What a joy that was. I know Tesco online does it now but somehow it's just not the same. The men bringing all that bounty became a part of my life. Spotty Chops, the rather horrible nickname of the boy who delivers the bread, would also solemnly hand over a lock of his hair once a month in an envelope – my grandmother is curing his warts and it requires hair and silver from him (the silver was a sixpence which was then buried in the garden at a full moon). I don't know if his cure worked. I hope it did or he could well have been snipped bald as well as being afflicted with a wart. Cheese, eggs, watercress, fish, onions, milk, shrimp ... they are all delivered on allotted days.

Even now, when the watercress I buy comes from a

supermarket and clearly states on the front 'washed and ready to eat', I wash and wash and wash it. Like Lady Macbeth, I can't stop washing. The fear of god was put in me by my grandmother of the dangers of fluke worms. One tiny egg was all it took and this monstrous thing would swell and grow and turn your skin blue and you would bloat and burst like balloon and never, ever go to a ballet class ever, *ever* again.

Such gore was pretty standard fare in our house, gruesome illness being a favoured topic of tea time conversation. I once saw a black and white educational film about leprosy and was convinced that I'd contracted it. In the film a man in a white coat, working under strenuous conditions in Africa, examines his wrists under a light and is horrified to discover he's got white spots. It's the first sign. I was trusted to wash alone by now in the bathroom and for weeks gaily ran the hot tap making splashing sounds. One fateful day, I too had the dreaded white spots. I ran breathlessly to my grandmother, determined to be brave, you understand, but also to let her know gently that I was not long for this world. She assured me drops of hot water on the skin of a very dirty little girl had quite the same appearance. Soap was called for. I limped off to the bathroom feeling obscurely cheated.

Grace Helen could be intimidating. Matilda Mary Anne was just plain scary.

She was my paternal grandmother and ran The Robin Hood pub in the East End of London with guts and gusto. She needed them. The East End in the 1960s was a dangerous place, not the trendy urban hub it is now. Her husband, my grandfather, was a gold miner. He worked six months of the year in what was then called the 'white man's graveyard'. The day he left for Africa again, her fancy man, Pineapple Jack, moved into the pub. He only left the day my grandfather came home six months later. This continued for decades, right up until my grandfather died, much to the general disapproval of Grace Helen. Then Pineapple Jack moved in for good. ('A most unsatisfactory arrangement,' said she with a sniff.)

Matilda Mary Anne was vivid in the extreme – loud colours and dripping jewellery added to the general *unsatisfactory* flavour of her. She reminded me of a parrot, same gaudy colouring and a beaky, slightly predatory look to her face. She once bought me a frilly nylon (v. modern, or so *I* thought) party dress of mauve and purple net, a small biscuit iced gem of a dress that scratched my legs. Grace Helen and my mother were mortified by it. I loved it. My normal party attire ran along the lines of silk and cotton so this peacock like garb was a new sensation to me. I flounced to show it off in front of everyone and heard Grace Helen say to my mother, 'Dear God, she looks like a bar maid!' while fanning her face with her hands. I later got into trouble by asking Matilda Mary Anne what low tastes meant.

Very occasionally my parents visit the Robin Hood. I am paraded behind the bar for the regulars to swoon over then whisked upstairs by my mother. Memories of men in coats nursing pint jars of stout and a piano being battered to death with Matilda Mary Anne seemingly the only woman there are all I have of it. That and the smell: stale beer, smoke and something else, maybe danger. Even now it seems very attractive.

5

What is definitely *not* attractive is jellied eels. I think they were my first gastronomic horror. I positively hated them. I can still see them glistening in a thick white china bowl with hot vinegar splashed over them. I hated them so much that I spat them clear across the room to land in a quivering globule against the canary yellow skirting board of my grandmother's upstairs parlour. My mother laughed, probably relieved that I didn't have low tastes after all.

Coming home from the pub, wrapped in a blanket in the back of the car, I listen drowsily to my parents talk. I *adored* being in that car, a Jaguar, I think. It had walnut flaps fitted in the back of the front seats that could be pulled down to create tables and was upholstered in pale blue leather. It even smelled safe. The voices from the front are muffled but clear enough to understand.

'Darling, she doesn't look well, you know.'

My father didn't reply. He often didn't reply, especially when he was driving or doing the cryptic crossword in the Times. This was a red rag to my mother who once set light to his paper to provoke a response. I reassured myself that she obviously couldn't ignite anything now because he was at the wheel. I heard her slide a cigarette out of its packet and the quick sulphurous strike of a match. Piccadilly Plain. That's what she smoked and she always lit the end of the cigarette that had the small writing on it. The other week I had asked why she did this. Giving me a slow smile she explained it made it harder for the police to trace her. *Deeply* thrilling.

'She's perfectly all right.'

I didn't quite understand the tone in his voice. It wasn't

something I'd heard before. Not angry, but somehow hard.
A sharp, flinty tone. I wondered if it had anything to do with
what I'd found out from Grace Helen. There was no love lost
between the two grandmothers and I had thrilled to the secret
that she had told me, though it had seemed very puzzling to
me at the time. My father was born in the pub. Matilda Mary
Anne had gone upstairs after locking the doors and delivered
him alone. She was so furious to discover that he was a boy,
she simply decided to call him Susan and dress him as a girl.
I had seen pictures of my father with long curly blonde hair,
ringletted and tied with a ribbon and wearing a long white
lacy dress. This hadn't struck me as odd, because it all seemed
so long ago, and I assumed that all small children were dressed
alike. I'd seen the faded sepia prints. They were just pictures.
I simply couldn't connect the faded images to my family. No
one knew. No one but her ever changed a nappy or bathed
him. Then the unthinkable happened. When he was seven the
school authorities carried him kicking and screaming from
behind the bar and dumped him at a school. He came home
with a shaved head, hobnail boots and knee length shorts.
My grandmother thought of the worst name that she could
and he was promptly christened Archibald William Thomas.
She suspected the landlady of The Grapes had had a hand in
it and from then on war was declared. By all accounts my
father turned into a ragamuffin overnight and was often
escorted home by the local policeman.

'Well, the place is too much for her.' My mother sounds
exasperated.

My father snorts derisively. 'You're not suggesting that
she –'

'No, no of course not. I just *worry*, that's all.'

That's true, I sleepily thought. My mother could worry for England. Dangers were lurking in every corner, even innocent looking women at Charing Cross station were actually in thrall to white slavers who would stab a small blonde girl with a hypodermic and bundle her into a laundry basket to wake up in some harem in the desert, the plaything of a pasha. I used to dream occasionally of silken tents in the desert and picture myself an Arab princess being presented with barbaric looking headdresses. Sadly no such thing ever happened, however pleadingly I stared at startled lone lady shoppers.

The car swooped round a corner and I slid along the back seat clutching at the tartan rug covering me.

'Bloody fool,' I heard my father mutter at another car, 'And look, he's wearing a hat! What have I always said? Never trust a man who drives in a hat.'

This was a given diktat, along with many others that made no sense whatsoever. All front doors must be painted scarlet. Never cut your nails with scissors, always clippers. Pimms can only be drunk in the afternoon. Cucumbers must always be peeled. And if a man asks you to dance, even if he is a halitosis ridden hunchback with maniacal tendencies, you must always accept. Even as a child I clearly remember wondering if all these things were really true and what would happen if you ever painted your door blue. The front door of my first home was painted crimson – as have all the others. As should all front doors.

My mother opens a window slightly and I can smell London is fading away. We will soon be home. If I fake sleep

8

I'd be carried up to bed but then I would miss out on a goodnight kiss from Grace Helen and a bon-bon. These were kept in a lignum vitae box, on a night stand and were slipped to me as if they were love letters. Covered with white icing sugar, they were a mixture of nuts, hard toffee and cinnamon. Perhaps not awfully pleasant really, but familiar and ritualistic.

The following day the house is in uproar. It seems Matilda Mary Anne has died in the night. Pineapple Jack rings to say that he found her slumped over the bar, a glass of rum in her hand.

Grace Helen is *delighted*. She makes the almost unheard of effort to climb into her bathchair and be wheeled into the kitchen to supervise the funeral dinner, preparations for which seem to be starting immediately.

A massive ham is being soaked in cold water, walnuts and almonds are being shelled – a fiddly, laborious job that is deemed suitable for small agile fingers, despite the many tears it provokes with squashed fingers in the very dangerous nutcrackers. I am quite happy with the job though, as it is reasoned to be grown up, which is my strongest wish. Pastry is made by my mother who is, without question, the lightest hand in that department.

The flow of chatter and laughter belie the fact that we are creating a funeral meal. Perhaps that's what happens then, when you die, everyone gets together and laughs their heads off?

My father strides around the kitchen quoting something from Hamlet about funeral baked meats. He seems rather delighted too.

Drinks are poured. It is, after all, an *event* – something

worth noting with the popping of a cork. My mother looks doubtful, 'Champagne? So early?' My father and Grace Helen exchange looks. Complicit, amused, gleeful almost. I am allowed a thimbleful. Of course, I milk the moment by pretending to be drunk and stagger round the kitchen with a rolling gait and end up flopped over Dobbin. Dobbin is an extremely beautiful Edwardian horse galloped free from a carousel. He has a gold barley twist pole floating up from his saddle and is gaily painted with scarlet flared nostrils. Of late he's become a bit of a dumping ground for jackets and coats and I feel guilty that I have neglected him a smidgen. But, after all, I am very nearly grown up and he is a bit, just a tad perhaps, too childish for me. I give an imitation hiccup and Grace Helen observes that I might make my fortune on the stage.

My mother starts to sing Burlington Bertie/I rise at ten thirty. My father smiles and catches her round the waist and they execute what looks like a remarkably polished soft shoe shuffle around the floor. Grace Helen and I are happy to see this and I seize this opportunity of family love to sneak another thimble of champagne, which is noted by my grandmother, but smiled upon. Parties are pretty common in our household but this one has me in a fever of excitement. I sense somehow, as all children do, that this is somewhat different. Endless deliveries constantly interrupt this fascinating, out of the ordinary morning, and soon all sorts of people are in the kitchen, leaning on the huge scrubbed table and remarking with pleasure at seeing Grace Helen out of bed.

I little know the effort its cost her but I am aware of my mother's anxious glances.

Incomprehensible chatter flows over me but I am used to this and sift various words and phrases out to mull over later.

Wills, probate, inheritance, cremation, burial plots, wreaths – all a mystery, but undoubtedly adult, and therefore to be treasured. The words get muddled with the smell of angelica that my mother is chopping and the rhythmic sound of a balloon whisk beating heavy cream in a copper bowl that Grace Helen is cradling in her lap. My father is opening another bottle, disregarding the protests of the watercress man who pleads that he has many more deliveries to make.

'Nonsense! A little liquid sunshine never harmed a soul,' my mother smiles at him. He falls under her spell and manfully drinks. He'd probably prefer a beer, but there is only champagne.

The day passes in a blur of golden bubbles. I have more and more thimbles of liquid sunshine and go to bed that evening undoubtedly quite drunk.

The following day I am furious to discover I am not going to the funeral. I am – can you believe it – too young. Oh, the indignity of being a child. What do they think I'm going to do? My mother dismisses the problem by saying that I have nothing black to wear, as if that is final. Even Grace Helen agrees with her. I swathe a black silk shawl around me and parade in front of them.

'Ridiculous, you look like Pola Negri,' my father sounds amused though, and is tempted to allow me to go, I can tell. But I know that it's hopeless. My mother and grandmother's word is the law – they decide what happens in our house. I give her my special look, and she squeezes my hand. 'No darling, really.' Then she adds something about me having quite enough funerals to attend when I am older and that it is not, after all, a party.

It *feels* like a party.

I am fobbed off with staying at home with Grace Helen. To prove how grown up I am, I accept my defeat gracefully but refuse to disrobe from the black heavily fringed shawl which I trip over with every stubborn step.

The house is swimming with the aroma of the ham. Cooked in cider, it is now cool and has been rubbed with mustard and muscovado sugar and studded with cloves. Pushing the cloves in was my job and has left tiny stigmata on the ball of my right thumb. They match the general yellow staining of the rest of my fingers caused by the blanching and peeling of what seemed like a ton of almonds for the legendary Tipsy Cake.

This cake, more a trifle really, is always prepared for family get-togethers. A lavish concoction of vanilla flecked custard, whipped cream, brandy, sherry, fruit and ratifer biscuits are melded together, and then, and only then, am I allowed to stud the top with slivered almonds. They stand up in a haphazard jumble, like pearly teeth, studding the yellow Jersey cream.

I hold the almonds in one hand and, with the tip of my tongue between my teeth, carefully place the last almond on the massive pudding.

Grace Helen and I gaze in silence at the perfection of it.

'Too good for her. Still, the family's coming,' Grace Helen says, with grudging satisfaction. She pins my still-sliding shawl into some semblance of a dress and we move regally into the dining room: me following the sagging creaking, wicker chair on wheels that she guides so expertly over the flagstoned floor of the kitchen and hall. We pause at the doorway. She gives a sigh of relief that everything is just so.

The long, white robed table is positively groaning under the weight of the food. Dark green ivy (considered a suitably funereal plant) trails through the stacks of plates entwining itself in the waiting silver cutlery. The ham, on the bone, with a frilly white paper rosette, holds centre stage. Some rosy slices have already been cut, ready to tempt the grief ridden hordes. The platters of kedgeree loan the room a slight aroma of curry, taking me away from a cold Kentish England to a warmer, sunnier land that I have only ever seen in encyclopaedias and heard distant relatives talk distantly of. Crumbling, flaky cheese straws dusted with cayenne pepper hold their long twisted shape on willow pattern platters. I see the few that I have twisted, which are not as perfect as the others but which have lovingly been given pride of place anyway.

Serried rows of cut glasses stand to attention. There will be sherry or gin and tonics for the Aunts and whisky for the men. Perhaps, afterwards, there will be wine too, or maybe punch. But no, I reason, if that were to happen, the battered silver punch bowl would already have been polished. Standing alone, amongst the grave looking wine bottles, is the unlikely outsider of a bottle of beer. Pineapple Jack. I catch Grace Helen's eye and she sniffs.

We have time for a game of snap before they arrive. She gives her finger tips a final buff with a nail file (all the better to detect the aces and royals she has doctored with pin pricks – 'cheating' was considered a nasty word). We settle down to the furious, high speed game. The cards dance from Grace Helen's hands, making the diamonds flash on her swollen fingers. The customary shouts and accusations fill the air. We are still clutching our sides from laughing, over a particularly close call with two jacks, when the cortège arrives. 'I won!' Grace Helen triumphantly announces. 'I shall be expecting your marker by the usual channels in due course.' This was my cue to say that my banker would be in contact with her banker. Honour satisfied, we brace ourselves for the onslaught. Anticipation grips my insides, the party has finally started.

Forty years on, those diamonds are on my fingers. I love giving a party, even a wake, and I always cheat at cards. One friend points out that cheating is a nasty name for a nasty business — Grace Helen's grand-daughter grandly dismisses this idea as ridiculous. Matilda Mary Anne wasn't all low tastes. She left me her gold jewellery (fashioned from red gold mined by my grandfather). She also bequeathed me an empty tortoiseshell, the unfortunate inhabitant of which, she always claimed, had been eaten by my grandfather, saving his life when he was lost in the African bush. I now use it as a doorstop. To the kitchen, of course.

Chapter 2

A Perilous Picnic with the Aunts

Home Made Lemonade
(there's no other kind)

6 lemons
8 tablespoons of castor sugar
2 pints of water

Thinly peel the lemons, leaving behind as much of the white pith as you can. Cover the peel with water and bring to the boil. Discard the water and repeat. On the third boiling, add the sugar and the water. Let the sugar dissolve and remove from the heat. Squeeze the juice from the remaining lemons and add. Taste for sweetness. Chill. Enjoy.

Grace Helen has sisters: Ruth, Ella and Margaret and another nameless two that come and go from various parts of the world. They all look alike – enormous busts, swathes of chestnut hair, slim ankles and determined chins. When I was very small I found it hard to tell them apart. They move like a fleet of liners docking in a foreign port – determined to show off their Englishness. They are all widowed and childless. They even all smell the same – a mixture of orris root powder, humbugs, tweed and violets. So you can but imagine how I am treated. I like to think of it as *indulged*, not spoilt. To say I am the apple of their eye does not convey the amount of love that flows over me. I am their treat, their doll, their angel, their star, their *life*.

They all adore holidays but loathe the journey (or do they?). It is hard for Grace Helen who is the eldest, and bedridden, to be left behind. Postcards arrive from far flung places that she reads longingly. She received one from France, after an especially bad crossing, from her sister Ella, that simply read: 'I thank god that I am an English woman, born in wedlock and that my feet are now on dry land!'. I could always use postcards to prompt tales of her travels to me – I'd heard them all before but it mattered not. Some were true, some were imagined? I could never tell the difference and didn't care. My mother, Joan, inherited this fabulous quirk and came to regale my primary school with a talk – 'Meanderings of a Memsahb'. How we all thrilled to the tales of soldier ants biting straight through a dining table, the rogue elephant that marauded the camp, the rainy season in the hills. I was the envy of the school. I hung on every word and asked what had happened to her first husband, the captain.

'It was very tragic darling, thank you for asking. A man eating tiger. *Awful* business. I don't like talking about it, really.'

I was about fifteen before I realised that she'd never set foot in India.

The well-travelled but avowedly travel-shy Aunts have a terrible fondness for picnics. It really doesn't matter what time of the year it is. Snow on the ground? A flask of apricot

brandy and a hunk of fruitcake and they are off, trailing
Liberty print scarves and fur tippets. This al fresco eating
is considered healthy, adventurous and – above all – *English*.

And so one hot summer's day Ruth and Ella swoop down
on me. I am quite contentedly making rose petal perfume
in the garden, stripping the petals off the sweetest smelling
flowers and bruising them in a pestle and mortar, then
soaking them in an enamel jug of water. This supposed elixir
was later to be bottled and 'sold' to my mother and Grace
Helen. (God, the perfumes that they both wallowed in.
Guerlain, Rochas, all in beautiful bottles with fantastically
lyrical names.)

The two Aunts have packed a hamper and are raring to
go. But where? On such a hot day woods or water are called
for. We set off in the car in a cloud of cheroot smoke (Ruth)
and violet pastels (Ella). I wave goodbye to my mother, and
notice Grace Helen mouthing something at the window. It
looks very much like 'it's going under' but this makes no
sense so we all wave and smile and promise to bring back
some wild flowers that she adores.

En route we stop to pick up Freddy. Freddy is a constant
fixture and a joy to be around, although I have no idea who
he actually *is*. Not a relation, certainly, but he is always at
every gathering and greeted with cries of delight by all the
Aunts and my mother (not *quite* as welcomed by the men,
perhaps.) A tall, slightly stooped man with faded hair, who
always smells delicious. A bit of a dandy, with smooth
manicured hands and a fund of scurrilous stories. It is hinted
that he is no longer welcome at Monte Carlo or Venice, due
to some ancient scandal involving him in a ladies' frock, but

this seems improbable to me. Why would anyone get into trouble about something so trivial as dressing up? When it comes to charades, or fancy dress parties, Freddy and I always squabble over the choicest clothes. An old Etonian, he speaks with a slight stutter and has a nice line in self deprecatory wit, that I recognise as the height of sophistication.

'So, Freddy, what news?' the Aunts demand.

'The raspberries are ripe, my summer suits *still* fits me, and I *ber ber*, *beat* Grace Helen last night at cards, what could be nicer?'

The Aunts titter appreciatively.

Freddy whispers to me, 'I *let* her win, you know, she really is a devil, isn't she?'

He raises an eyebrow at me and I delightedly pat his jacket pockets till I find the tin of moustache wax that he keeps there. I smear some on the tips of my fingers, and carefully wax the tips of his moustache.

'Ah, that's better, thank you dear girl, a light hand. Finer than the Turkish *ber ber barbers* in Alexandria. Ever been? No, well you should. Perhaps we'll go together.'

'On my birthday?' I plead.

He considers. 'Hmm, a possibility I should say, a definite possibility. Mind you, are we prepared? Hmm? Shots and things to be considered – not to mention mosquito nets, visas, all sorts of things. Quinine, that's what we'll need. *Ber ber* better ask your father.'

I promise to do so and, even though the exchange is purely rhetorical, I spend the rest of the journey rapturously thinking of Freddy and I jaunting around Egypt.

We bump and lurch through fields and down dirt tracks, passing the weir where *very naughty* and *very silly* children are splashing about in dangerous water (I glance scornfully at them, poor things, they don't have the Aunts to protect them), finally arriving at our destination and unpacking the car. Freddy collapses onto a groundsheet, fanning a silk handkerchief to cool his face, whilst the Aunts fuss over the food. It is a blisteringly hot day, cloudless and motionless. The trees bend to the sullen river and even the swans are too hot to glide around haughtily reading their own fan mail. Freddy puts his Panama over his eyes and directs me to wake him when the Hock is cool enough. I edge the long necked green bottle carefully into the water and secure it with some string and stones.

The Aunts light a primus stove for tea. A picnic is unthinkable without this foul smelling bit of apparatus, as I am well aware. My job is to unwrap the greaseproof packages of sandwiches which I identify by smell. Cucumber, of *course*, the cucumber salted and soaked in vinegar, the crusts neatly cut off. Miss Robinson's mock crab – a mixture of grated cheese and onion and vinegar (who Miss Robinson was, I really don't know and never found out). Gentleman's Relish, egg and cress, a bunch of hot radishes and a twist of salt. A cos lettuce wrapped in a damp blue and white checked tea towel. Raspberries, cherries – I pick out the double stemmed ones and loop over Freddy's ears and my own as living jewellery and, oh joy, a sponge cake. Finally, homemade lemonade just for me.

Sometimes there is a surprise in the picnic – most extravagantly and delightfully a pot of caviar, to be eaten with an agate spoon. (I really didn't enjoy it very much, but I grasped that it was expensive, and adult, and therefore *made* myself enjoy it. Of course, then, having faked it, I really did grow to love it.)

I creep up behind Freddy with a long stalk of grass and gently swish it under his nose, he obligingly pretends that it is a fly and swishes me away. I assure him that the wine is cool now and he consents to join the party.

I have noticed that Freddy never does any of the work on these outings, leaving it all to the Aunts, which is strange because my father is always doing the work but somehow Freddy just doesn't. I sense that he is somehow *different* from other men and accept this. He is also always surrounded by women, as is my father, but they respond to him in a very different way. The Aunts flutter round my father, shooting looks at him from their green cat's eyes, demanding his advice on their investments, their new cars or the health of their dogs. They place a charm braceletted wrist on his arm, when he pours them a drink, and smile their thanks up at him, with lowered head and wide eyes. With Freddy, they boss him about slightly and laugh. A lot. They also talk about clothes. A *lot*. For Freddy is the arbiter of taste and knows exactly how a scarf should be draped or the angle of a hat. Ella is wearing a straw hat with a green ribbon wrapped around the crown, far back on her head. Freddy says it makes her look like the village idiot, and jams it firmly down on her brow.

I recline on the flattened grass pretending that I am a vestal virgin being served by acolytes in a Greek temple. I have absolutely no idea what a virgin *or* an acolyte is but I like the sound of the words. I am stuffed but I cannot resist the damp salty sandwiches. I know that there is a cake, too, but that can wait. I gulp down the cloudy lemonade, which is the nicest drink imaginable on a hot day, blending the sharp with the sweet, and stare up at the canopy of green leaves above my head.

The Aunts and Freddy chatter away, as they always do, and I pick out the words that I shall want explained later. It's pointless to interrupt and demand an explanation now, it only makes them lose the thread. I roll over and examine the micro world of ants, where I can play god, creating walls and bridges for them to cross. Feeling benevolent, I feed them tiny crumbs of bread and watch them signal madly that there is a feast available.

Out of nowhere Grace Helen's storm arrives. It is suddenly as dark as night. The thunder and lightning are terrifying — cracking the still summer air. There are no rain drops, only sheets of solid water. We grab what we can and hurl ourselves in the car. Freddy holds me tightly on his lap. I hear him mutter, 'Too biblical, really. The Almighty really does have a taste for the matinee. What next? A *per per plague* of locusts?'

The Aunts are delighted with this turn of events and are, for once, stunned into silence at the deluge. It really is impossible to talk anyway because the storm is so loud. A clap of thunder has me wriggling for the safety of Freddy's chest and he squeezes me ever more tightly.

'No fear, old thing. Safest place to be, a car.'

With these words, we all feel the car begin to move. Slowly, but inexorably, it glides down the slippery wet bank towards the river.

'Girls, girls, the handbrake!' Freddy shouts.

But it is too late. The Aunts are transfixed by the situation and by the time they scrabble wildly for the brakes we are in the river, nose down, the current tugging at the small car.

Freddy and the Aunts start to laugh.

'Safest place to be, Freddy, hey?' The Aunts splutter between tears of laughter.

I am frightened but reassured that they find this funny. I look out of the window and see the swans next to me. I start to laugh too.

We finish what remains of the picnic in the car turning very gently to and fro in the current. The swans circle us, puzzled at the loud non-stop laughter issuing from this strange animal in their water. Our laughter can probably be heard in the next water meadow.

We are marooned in the river and must while away the time till we are rescued, or one of the Aunts braves the water. Freddy points out that it is impossible for him to as kind Mrs Jaeger would be very upset with him. Instead he regales us with tales of his golden youth and golden youths. Days and nights when he had the pick of the crop and turned every manly head on the Lido. We tuck our feet up on the seats to keep them out of the swirling water that has seeped into the car and listen. I am seven and the Aunts and Freddy have a combined age of two hundred and thirteen. I discover that I like Hock and divine the true meaning of virgin. Freddy explains. It means a boy who has never eaten cherries.

To this day I have an abiding love of food eaten outside. I hope that every picnic turns into an adventure. I am still old fashioned about picnic food and have been known to get misty eyed just at the sight of grease proof paper. No cling film for me! I have always had a 'Freddy' in my life and feel sorry for people who don't. I have inherited from the Aunts certain very English qualities: pluck, acceptance of things and people as they are, 'making the best of', laughing at one's own calamities and a firm belief that finding the humour in everything is a justifiable quest. And, of course, the recipe for homemade lemonade.

Chapter 3

The Uncles or Any Spoon
Will Do...

Smoked Trout Pâté

1 smoked trout
Good dollop crème fraiche
Dollop of cream cheese
Dollop horseradish sauce
Handful of chopped parsley
Juice and grated zest of 1 lemon

Remove bones and skin of trout, and then whiz all ingredients together. (You could also use a pestle and mortar – very effective to relieve aggression.) Chill the pate and serve with hot granary toast.

My mother has two brothers: John, the eldest, and Michael, the baby of her family. They breeze in and out of my life. They all have the Borkett nose (and the older I get, I realise I have it too, *not* something I am overjoyed about). The Uncles are small, quick witted men. They are charismatic to such a degree that I find myself standing as close to them as I can possibly get, trying to absorb their essence. Perhaps some of their magnetism will rub off on me? Maybe it's catching, like chicken pox (only fun)?

Michael leads a charmed life, so it seems. Wealthy and successful with an impossibly thin, tall elegant wife who buys Vogue and lives in Hampstead and eats artichokes. They are *posh*. Their house has all sorts of things that ours does not: Staffordshire figurines, pot pourri, a housekeeper, central heating, phones in *every* room, bath oil, wine racks, and a whole wall of LPs. The inventory is endless and intoxicating.

Our house is very different. Older, shambolic and *cold*. Coal fires in the downstairs rooms and ice in the water glass at night. The kitchen is the only room that is truly warm.

We drive to Hampstead for Sunday lunch, my mother hugging herself in the knowledge that both brothers will be there. My father, innocently driving in the days before breathalysers, is happily anticipating the wine. They have a Great Dane, Danny, that I bridle and lead like an unwilling but biddable pony around their walled garden.

We arrive and crunch down the drive.

John, Joan and Michael all talk so much and laugh so much that no one else can get a word in. That's OK, we all listen, entranced. More people arrive, and amongst them is a woman with those flinty eyes that clearly say 'I do *not* like children'. She stands very close to the Uncles and I am darkly jealous. I glance at my mother and she tips me a wink. So, she's seen it too. The woman throws her head about a lot when she gives her high pitched laugh and places her hand on Michael's arm to emphasise just how funny he is. I am *furious*. It takes all my control and grown up behaviour not to kick her. I stare at her with faux innocent eyes, willing her to disappear.

I retire to the corner of the room, stroking Danny, the better to study this woman. She is constantly playing with her hair and lowering her eyes to give sultry glances to the men. Her laugh is piercing. It could surely shatter glass at three paces. It's a bray. I brood and decide that, no matter what, I am never, *ever* going to be like that when I grow up. She flutters between Michael and John, who, I notice, much to my gratification, are being polite but no more. My father seems to find her fascinating. *Surely* he can't. He fills her glass and she positively wriggles with delight. She starts a long, boring anecdote, that my father listens attentively to then she stops abruptly saying, 'Whoops, I'd better not go on, there are young ears here after all!' (BRAY!) I give her my best scornful stare. I am impotent with the curse of childhood. I feel like assuring her that I've heard it all before, I am an old hand at grown up conversation – you have to be when you're an only child. Besides what does she think *she* could possibly say that I haven't heard before? I resume my brooding, Byronic (so I think) stare. My mother saunters towards me and whispers, 'She's nothing but a silly trout, ignore her darling.' I laugh and feel better.

Summonsed to lunch I am put in pride of place between the two Uncles. I allow myself a victory smile of satisfaction at the discountenance of the Trout. She is *most* put out. She begins boring for England again on the subject of small children ruining meals. My mother shoots looks at me and I squirm slightly in my chair. How to overcome this fury at being so unfairly treated? I am *always* on best behaviour at meal times. Doesn't she know that I am just as wanted here as she is? More so. I wrack my brains for something witty and grown up to say that will put her firmly in her place and shut her up.

I glance at the plate being put before me and I am flummoxed. I don't know what it is. A starter of some sort. Not only do I not recognise the food I don't know what to eat it with. Panic sets in. I know that I am meant to start on the outside of a place setting and work inwards, but surely this can't be right? There is a small spoon and a fork on the outside and this, whatever it is, surely needs a knife? I can feel a hot blush of red start to sweep my face. Oh god, now the Trout will know that I really *am* a child and not versed at all on the etiquette of dining with adults.

As if by magic, the Trout is lured to my discomfort. My mother is too far away to help me. A tiny part of my mind somehow knows that this is a trivial incident, but the majority of my brain is screaming for help and revenge. In that order.

The Trout fakes a smile at me and very slowly mimes picking up the small fork, then the small spoon from the side of her plate. Patronising, insulting, braying *whinnying* old witch! I fume, willing my blush of shame to fade.

Uncle John catches this exchange and swoops swiftly to rescue my pride. He grabs an oversized serving spoon from the centre of the table and scoops his entire starter into it and then, leaning across me, clownishly feeds it to his brother. 'I find any spoon will do!' he cries. In the second of surprised silence that follows this, I spoil the moment of triumph by tossing my hair about and imitating the woman's very high, very loud, shrill laugh. Not funny, and *not* clever, I know.

28

I've been told. Though I did have the satisfaction of making both Uncles snort with suppressed laughter.

About five years later, early in the morning, on my twelfth birthday the front door chimes. I open it, sticky handed clutching toast and marmalade. The Uncles are standing in the doorway. Both of them. I immediately suspect the worst: war must have been declared overnight or surely someone has died. There can be no other explanation. Michael should surely be at work (something quite mysterious in the *City* connected with advertising). John practically lived in a foreign country (Cumberland). I gape at them. They regard me solemnly.

'What *are* you wearing, for Chrissake?' Michael says at last, quite irritably.

I glance downwards. To be fair, it *is* spectacularly horrid. A school uniform of navy blue box pleated tunic, a powder blue shirt (buttons missing) and long white socks.

'Won't do at all,' John says, taking the toast from my hand and calling for my mother, 'Run along and get changed, you've got about twenty minutes.'

I narrow my eyes at them, do they actually *know* it's my birthday? Maybe not. I've learnt a bit about men by now and recognise that women are the ones who remember dates and the like. I see no gift wrapped present. Do they even know I have to go to school? Something that my mother and I have already had words about – 'Yes, darling I agree, birthdays *should* be special. No you can't stay at home reading. Yes, school is *quite* horrid, I'm sure. No, you can't leave at fifteen. Because we love you and want you to go to University. You *will* like it. It will *not* be like school. You'll go because

29

you won't want to spend your days cleaning the loos at Charing Cross station. No, I've told you, it's quite different from school – you'll like it. You will. You *will*. You will plus one to infinity. And beyond. Shut *up*.'

'Where are we going?' I ask tentatively.

'Paris. Birthday lunch, now hurry *up*.'

The Uncles silence my mother's rather half hearted protests and I fly up the stairs, ripping off my hated uniform (I have an aversion to navy blue to this very day). The Uncles have been up all night, playing poker. They won. They have *hired* a four seater plane. To take *me* to *Paris*. I am in seventh heaven. I am alone with the Uncles going to *Paris*. I think I might die of happiness.

The Uncles are swigging great mugs of tea and lighting cigarettes in the kitchen, regaling my mother with the night's adventures. I can tell that she's delighted for me but also worried. Of *course*. We could all crash in the plane or get food poisoning – something that only happens *abroad*. My Uncles might lose me, white slavers are far more prolific in Paris, it stands to reason. They laugh at her and sweep me into the waiting car. We wave goodbye and *at last*, my grown up days are here, surely?

One minute I am in the kitchen. The next I am in Paris.

They take me to *Julien*, that airy, romantic Belle Époque restaurant on the rue du Faubourg Saint Denis. The Uncles are by now hungover, tired and faintly disagreeable to each other and only imperceptibly nicer to me. It matters not. I am silenced by the room. The art nouveau décor is stunning. And sexy. It is Paris in the mid Sixties and chic beyond words. Two women are having lunch together with their

30

two white poodles sitting next to them on chairs, places
laid. Waiters have long white aprons tied behind their waists
and move so fast it seems they are on roller skates. Oysters
are being slurped at the next table by a man who is beyond
glamour: he has stubble, is wearing dark glasses and has a
trench coat slung over his shoulders. A Gauloise smoulders
in his ashtray. I am in love. I wonder if I can make him
notice me. (Ah, cherie, ze first time I saw you, you were
but a child, but I knew zen zat I must 'ave you. I will wait
until you are sixteen, no more.) A menu is proffered and I
am entranced by the list of words that I know *must* be food
– but what? John and Michael perk up when the champagne
arrives. They toast me, and, oh joy and embarrassment, the
man on the next table raises his glass to wish me a *bon
anniversaire*. I manage what I think to be a knowing smile
of sophistication. Dear Uncle John whispers that I look at
least fourteen and should he slip the blighter at the next
table my address? I glow with pride.

Michael insists that as it is my birthday I must order
whatever I want from the menu. The trouble is, I don't
know what I want. Caviar, *of course*. But none of it looks
familiar. I want something grand enough to warrant this
visit. Something memorable. What I get is an enormous
platter of *fruits de mer*. Things that God made as a joke,
surely? What is that huge shell, that's *moving* slightly on the
crushed ice? I sense that I must attack this with no
squeamishness so I tuck in with gusto. As do the Uncles.
Soon, the whole table is littered with pink langoustine
whiskers, blue black mussel shells and claws of all kinds.
The debris of the deep.

31

This feast is followed by an unfamiliar fish in a silky smooth sauce. What was it? Halibut? Monkfish? I can't remember. I probably didn't know. More champagne. I am in full flood now and have enough confidence to ask the waiter, in a schoolgirl French, for strawberries.

'*Avec crème fraiche?*'

I nod authoritatively, making my Uncles laugh. They skip the fruit but have a brandy. I sip at it and try my best to like it but I cannot.

We saunter down the Champs Elysées where they take me to Courèges and buy for me a black and white PVC raincoat that is, obviously, the epitome of chic. They also buy rather a lot of presents for their wives.

Back on the plane, the Uncles worry that I might be sick but decide that, as I have the Borkett blood in me, I will surely survive what turns out to be a very bumpy ride indeed, without throwing up. I am unbearable for weeks afterwards and insist on wearing the PVC coat around the house as a dressing gown.

Eight years after that lunch in Hampstead my father left home to go and live with the Trout. My instinct, as most children's are, was right. Nothing goes unnoticed by a jealous seven-year-old. Nothing.

The best birthday surprise in the world has never been beaten. Well, it wasn't. Not for forty years when I swapped the private plane and Paris for a certain very glamorous train and Venice. But we'll get to that. The complete *rightness* of taking a twelve-year-old somewhere memorable is not to be underestimated. I honestly think it changed my life. The ability to drop everything and go with the moment is a blessing. It also makes me a real pushover for the day off work, the long long lunch, the stolen moment – an escape from responsibility? Probably.

I also picked up a hint for the adventurous eater. Some things that look disgusting, probably are. But *sometimes* they're not. Like most things in life, the only way of knowing is to try. With gusto.

Chapter 4

Sunday Bloody Sunday

Bread Sauce

This is so easy, and so good, I cannot believe anyone buys it ready-made.

1 pint of milk
1 bayleaf
salt & black pepper
1 small onion or shallot studded with cloves
knob of butter
1 tbsp cream
breadcrumbs (probably about six thick slices,
whizzed up in the processor.
Before the advent of which, they were laboriously grated by
hand, and usually tinged red with the blood from my
knuckles. I use any bread I have in the kitchen, brown or
white, stale or fresh. The quantity depends on how much it
soaks the milk up, you may need more or less.)

Place onion, bayleaf & butter in the milk and simmer for about twenty minutes. Season well. Add breadcrumbs and stir in cream just before serving. DO NOT OVER-STIR – you want it to look textured, not like wallpaper paste.

Sundays as a child, were, on the whole, the most unutterably bloody days of the week. Desiccated, dead and predictable. A Victorian hangover when absolutely *nothing* was open. There were no friendly Asian run corner shops where you could pop in and get the papers, a pint of milk and a gooey bit of baklava.

There was the dread of school looming on Monday. But before that there was Church. Terrible. Terrible and boring. I am sent much against my will.

'It's *so* hypocritical, *you* never go,' I wail.

'I know darling, but it's best to get it over with now then, when you're grown up, you'll know what to do without looking around all the time. I feel so sorry for people who don't know what to do in church. If you go back with the vicar, be sure to steal a peach,' my mother answers vaguely, her nose deep in a book, a large breakfast cup dotted with swirling poppies steaming with hot tea and a cigarette smouldering in the ashtray beside her.

The vicar has a famed conservatory with peaches and muscatel grapes growing in it. The thrill of stealing from a *man of the cloth* makes the visits almost bearable. My mother doesn't go to church because she can't bear hymns. Neither can I, I protest, but that is swept aside. My father doesn't go because he plays cricket on a Sunday. That's even more boring than church, though I quite like the sleepy claps that echo round the field when he bowls someone out. He is a feared slow bowler and, being ambidextrous, can change his bowling arm at the last moment. Grace Helen never goes to church because she disapproves of something or other to do with the creed and by now she never leaves her bed. It

36

strikes me as extremely unjust that it is left to me to stake out the family place in heaven.

I sulk horribly, and professionally, as only small girls can. Before settling into a complete sulk I am persuaded to go with the promise of roast chicken on my return.

'*And* bread sauce?' I question suspiciously.

Reassured, I grudgingly set off.

It is, of *course*, raining. I daringly take the (forbidden) short cut to the church. It entails a walk down a deserted lane and through a field known as Hanging Meadow. I frighten myself enjoyably with imagined sightings of swinging bodies from tree tops. I note where mushrooms are growing, ready for me to pick on my return journey. Then, the deeply thrilling thought occurs to me. What happens if I just don't go? Will the sky fall in? Nah. *Probably* not. But what will I do? It's not cold but it's very wet.

I wade through knee high wet grass and sit under a beech tree. I hear the church bell hurrying the latecomers and I smile. Not today, thanks awfully. The grass is a deep lush emerald green, and the leaves above my head are dripping. I regret not thinking my plan out properly. I should have brought a book with me or somehow sneaked out Marmaduke, our large water loving retriever. How long does church last exactly? I have no idea. I don't have a watch and find telling the time laboriously, painfully difficult, despite lessons from Grace Helen. Does the church bell ring *after* the service? I can't remember.

All I really know is that I am delighted *not* to be in church. I feel deeply, thrillingly, wicked. A rather nice sensation. (It still is.)

If church was how it should be, I reasoned, I would go. It *should* be full of the holy ghost and magic. What it *is* full of is coughing old people, dusty pews and cloth backed prayer books that are falling apart. It is desperately short on laughs, though there was that time last summer when the vicar said a very rude word (albeit accidentally). It had been a hot day and as he climbed to the pulpit to give one of his tremendously *worthy* sermons – the cue for me to drift off, imagining I am the last descendant of the Tsar: the officials are anxiously attending my triumphant return, mislaid papers, swapped at birth, horrible mix up, diamonds and pearls await, we apologise your royal highness with all our hearts . . . We beseech you to take the throne, you will, won't you? Then the vicar, a large slightly sweaty man with a comb over, utters the immortal lines: 'If the gentlemen of the congregation find it as warm as I do, then please feel free to remove your jackets and shit in your sirtsleeves . . .'

Now that *was* funny. I regaled the family with it to much success, so much so that I was allowed to phone Uncle John in Cumberland and repeat it.

I pick a stalk of grass and chew the sweet white stem. The hour or so seems endless *and* wet. Nearly as boring as being in church but I can't back down now. I while the time away by staring at the trees and willing a miracle to happen to *prove* that there is a god. The sun makes a brief appearance, but even I can't count that.

Eventually I saunter home, ready to answer any possible questions about church. None are asked because we have had an unexpected visit from Michael and his wife, Dorothy. Best of all, they have brought Danny, their Great Dane, with them. Our dog and Danny *get on* and are tearing round the wet garden. Michael and my father are sitting on Grace Helen's bed sipping whisky.

I go into the kitchen, which is flooded with the delicious smells of roasting chicken, to find Dorothy perched on a chair, sipping an orange juice. She is, and always will be, impossibly tall, thin and glamorous. She wears the bespoke Moschino trouser suit that will cut a dash for decades to come. I kiss her hello and she asks where I've been.

My mother glances at me, as if somehow she just *knows* that I've been sitting in a soggy meadow, even though I take great care to keep the wet seat of my skirt turned away from her. This uncanny ability to spot a lie beggars belief. It also causes massive rows later on when I become that wild unruly thing – a teenager.

'Boring old church,' I say cheerfully, aware that this alone may cause a frisson of tension as my aunt is, alone amongst the family, a *Roman Catholic* (or 'filthy papist' as Grace Helen puts it). The whole concept of Catholicism is beyond me. I know it's something to do with Henry VIII and Jesus on the cross but what exactly I don't know. All I do know is that Dorothy has *nailed* Jesus to the cross on her bedroom wall. During Easter week one year I appeal to the arbiter of truth, Grace Helen, about this and she assures me that he is held in place with Sellotape and that all Catholics are wilfully deceived. I am very relieved and happily point this out to the vicar, who I imagine may well benefit from knowing the *truth*.

Because my aunt is a filthy papist she does odd things, like eating fish on a Friday and crossing herself occasionally.

This could well be the reason that she is drinking orange juice, I think. Perhaps some obscure saint's day requires it? My mother has a gin and tonic by her side and is seasoning the bread sauce with abandon.

'Just in time darling, I need a taster,' she says, holding out a wooden spoon.

Years later I am enchanted to discover that Noel Coward feels *exactly* the same way about bread sauce, ordering it faithfully every year with a free-range roasted chicken for his birthday lunch. It is worth noting that chicken wasn't the every day dish that it is now. Honestly, it did taste better then: tastier, gamier and more, well, *chickeny*.

The lunch is lovely with me getting all the treats (the oysters from the chicken, the crunchiest roast potatoes and more than my fair share of bread sauce – my mother never makes *enough*). No questions are raised about Church and I realise that I have *got away with it* – is there a nicer feeling in the world? I doubt it. All the adults seem in a very good mood and it is broken to me that Dorothy is expecting a baby. I am totally unimpressed and escape to the garden to play with the dogs.

Later that night, as I am sent to bed unreasonably early, in my view, noises of a party drift up from downstairs. They are playing *hats*, one of my favourite games. This arcane family caper involves the snatching of various headgear from heads and lots of leaping about. It can get very rowdy. The selection of hats varies from a fez through to a magical opera hat that lays flat until smartly tapped and then it miraculously springs open. My mother, wearing a bowler hat and a fake moustache, comes up to my bedroom with a consolation prize of a box of Ritz crackers and a glass of tonic water with a slice of lemon and two ice cubes. I try the well worn excuse that I have a slight tummy ache and that I might as well get up and join the party as school is probably out of the question tomorrow. I can see that she is swayed a little but not enough.

As the night progresses I hear my aunt stagger slightly through the library and down the long corridor that leads from our freezing bathroom. Is she drunk? Surely not, she was only sipping orange juice, because of the *baby*. Drunkenness fills me with curiosity. I can't say I have ever seen a *real* drunk but I know that when my family get together lots of booze is consumed and it *seems* to make them all very jolly. The fine line between slightly tipsy and completely pissed doesn't occur to me till many years later (when I stagger across it).

I hear her call out and I hesitate. Should I go and see what the matter is? Getting *out* of bed is frowned upon, I know. I hear her again and gingerly tip toe round the corner. What I see does not reassure me. I scurry downstairs. A *grown up* is needed.

Very soon the house is full of ambulance men. Despite his immense size, Danny is a nervy dog. Instantly he picks up on the anxiety and suffers spectacular diarrhoea in my parents' bedroom. *Our* dog, Marmaduke, is under the impression that the ambulance men are attempting to kidnap my aunt so growls and bites one of them, hard, in the ankle. In all the excitement I bite my tongue and blood drips down my chin. My father, in a poke bonnet, is trying to loosen Marmaduke's hold on the paramedic, loses his footing and crashes down the stairs. Dorothy, who is on a stretcher, clutches the banisters for support, perhaps not realising that years of wood worm have taken their toll. Grace Helen is calling from her room, demanding to be told what the hell is going on. Michael, still clutching his whisky and wearing a flowered apron and rubber gloves (he's been dealing with Danny's mess in the bedroom), tells the ambulance men to take the whole bloody family to casualty. My mother mops tears of hysteria from her face.

Some Sunday.

Dorothy tells me, years later, that the miscarriage was nothing to the embarrassment she suffered being accompanied in the ambulance by my mother still in a bowler hat and moustache, and Michael, who had snatched up a ladies' Ascot number complete with a blue velvet rose for the occasion.

I am, of course, found out for not going to church. My father says that if I don't want to go I don't have to go again. I don't. This surely is a miracle.

It is also gently broken to me by Grace Helen that *not* going to church and then *lying* about it has nothing whatsoever to do with the miscarriage. I look at her with great astonishment. It never occurred to me that it did.

The connection between something bad happening and me behaving in a way that some might say was bad has never occurred to me. Never – not then, not now. If God does exist (and I grudgingly accept she might) a small lie from me is not going to tilt the axis of the world to such an extent that anything – never mind something awful – might happen.

Only on recent Sundays have I been able to bear giving

the best bits of the chicken to someone else (my goddaughter Alice). And I *always* make more than enough bread sauce. You never know who might be inclined to drop in.

Chapter 5

Appley and Strawy

Chocolate Rose Leaves

Gather lots of rose leaves, shake free of any insects, gently wash and pat dry.

Melt a quantity of good plain chocolate and, with a paint brush, paint the underside of each leaf.

Spread the leaves on grease proof paper. When the chocolate has set, carefully peel off the rose leaves.

Voila! A perfect chocolate leaf. Very satisfying.

I am Appley and my mother is Strawy. I don't know why or how I came up with these names. But they stick. They are our cooking names: noms de chefs. I have an apron tied around me and stand on a tiny home made chair so that I can reach the work top and 'cook'. There always seems to be a lot of pastry involved. It's all made with a mixture of butter and Cookeen. What the hell was Cookeen? Some sort of lard? It sounds revolting, but it wasn't. A hint of grated lemon peel goes in the sweet pies.

Few of my friends now own a rolling pin but when I was young it seemed that every other meal was some form of pie necessitating the use of this instrument. Perhaps pies made the food go further? Savoury pies (chicken and leek, speckled with black pepper was a favourite) and, of course, all the fruit pies: apricot, rhubarb, blackcurrant and, in season after hours of getting scratched walking country lanes tin bowl in hand, blackberry and apple.

I am making a pie for Grace Helen with the off cuts of the pastry, which is now a very unappealing grey colour due to excessive handling from my dirty little paws. I carefully place dandelions and daisies in the middle of the pastry and, leaning with all my might, roll it hard into a ragged rectangle. I sprinkle this with sugar and Strawy places it in the scarily hot oven, that I have no need of telling *not* to touch.

This flower baking is not just childish fancy. Grace Helen *eats* flowers. No, really. Once, when she was hungry and lunch was late, she ripped the heads off two roses and a carnation from the vase beside her bed and wolfed them down with evident relish. She nibbles at early primroses with delight. At my mother's wedding Grace Helen was so anxious and peckish she ate her own corsage. It was made up of orchids which I think may have given her indigestion for she didn't recommend them.

Of course, it was drummed into me what was poisonous in the garden. I steered clear of laburnum, foxgloves and yew but all other plant life was well put to culinary and medicinal purposes. Some to great effect, some to none at all.

Foraging for food was always encouraged, most especially mushrooming. For this highly competitive sport a field was quartered and searched like police hunting for murder clues. Cries of delight went up whenever a prize was found. Some mushrooms were *deadly* poisonous (never just poisonous but *deadly*, this added a frisson of pleasure). A puffball was a

thing to briefly treasure before frying to a crisp in hot butter
with a tiny amount of finely chopped garlic and serving on
toast. I can taste it now but can't remember when I last
saw a puffball.

Sorrel, borage and nasturtium flowers for salad. Lavender
for ice cream. Big handfuls of wild garlic and sharp mint
for roast lamb. I was sent out to pick these things from the
garden and seldom made a mistake. Although I once came
back clutching three small laurel leaves, instead of bay, which
Strawy very nearly tossed into the casserole. Thank god she
checked first or we would all have been quite ill.

When the pie for Grace Helen comes out of the oven it
is obviously *not* a success but it is taken in to her and she
dutifully nibbles a crumb or two to keep me happy.

The afternoon darkens and rain lashes at the windows.
Grace Helen is tired and doesn't even want to play with
the devil's pictures: a sure sign of genuine tiredness as usually
the idea of a game of cards, even with a child, perks her
up no end. I turn to my mother for inspiration. She looks
out of the window at the cold wet day and smiles.

'Farting about in the kitchen, I think darling, don't you?'

I snort with laughter. Fart is one of those words that
although considered *quite* rude is nevertheless hysterically
funny. It has also come to take on a very different meaning
than its original one. Farting around means messing about,
not really doing anything much. 'Oh fart!' is an expression
that covers just about every emotion from mild annoyance
to amazed disbelief. It was once iced on a birthday cake for
me to great giggling success.

Strawy and I retreat to the kitchen to create chocolate

rose leaves. These have the advantage of being completely useless but very pretty. They can be stored in an air tight tin and later used to decorate cakes or as exotic petits fours. They are the *perfect* thing to make on a rainy afternoon with a bored child (or adult).

As we begin I beg Strawy to tell me about the war. I am fascinated by this subject and long to hear more about it. The Blitz, the Black Out, the rationing, gravy browning painted on as stockings, parachute silk snipped up and worn as underwear . . . the sheer excitement of it all seems thrilling beyond belief.

'Well, now let me think . . . You know the Gargoyle club?'

I give in immediately to the usual pretence that I am a contemporary and that I was with her during that time, and nod.

'Well, it was one evening in there and the air raid had just sounded. No one took much notice of it and we all carried on dancing. I remember it very clearly because Dylan Thomas was there, *not* his usual haunt of course but there you are. He was drunk, *of course*, and he'd just asked me to dance – none of us liked dancing with him, bad breath for a start, and he always asked to borrow money. Well, there was simply the most *enormous* explosion and the whole building shook. A bomb had fallen very, very close. I thought the club was going to collapse so rushed to the stairs and ran outside. Others took the lift, do you remember it? Small and made of glass – *very* dangerous, I thought. Anyway, I lost a shoe in the rush. Very pretty it was too: high heeled with a beautiful green flower on the toes. I was damned if I was going to let Hitler take one of my shoes so I stopped to find it. Goodness, people were rude! Pushing and pushing to get past me but I found it in the end and had just put it back on when there was another enormous explosion and the sound of crashing glass. The next thing I knew I was swept up in the arms of a man who ran down the stairs carrying me! We were simply covered in dust and rubble. When we got outside the whole street seemed to be on fire! He was still holding me and only then did I see who he was!'

I beg to know his identity. When it is given I am none the wiser. It is explained to me that he is a famous actor. I am suitably impressed.

'Oh yes, I saw him again. We dined together quite often. He was always broke, it really wasn't done then you know for the woman to pay for everything. I used to pay for his Guinness. That man still owes me more than a few drinks.'

We carefully pull off the chocolate which has set by now to reveal a miraculously perfect chocolate leaf complete with veins and jagged edges.

We are interrupted by the arrival of the egg man. (Years later when the Beatles hit came out I would answer the door with, 'hey hey it's the egg man,' and he would dutifully and solemnly reply, 'coo goo ga choo'.) He joins us for a cup of tea in the kitchen and admires our chocolate leaves.

He and Strawy talk more about the war. I listen carefully. I gather his war was nowhere near as much fun as my mother's. Tanks and deserts are discussed. It sounds *awful*. Metal so hot from the sun you could *fry an egg on it*. Half a finger missing from something called shrapnel. I gaze at him enraptured. I didn't know that we had a hero in the shape of the egg man. I ask him if he's got medals. He winks at me and says he'll bring them round next time to show me. I say he should wear them, all the time. He and my mother laugh.

They then start to talk about something called the black market.

'Oh, I remember positively *begging* for an onion,' my mother says, refilling the tea cups.

Begging for an *onion*? It's mystifying. Other things that I've never heard of come into the conversation such as powdered egg and rook pie. It doesn't sound very nice.

The egg man tells me that when he came home from the war his wife had hoarded some rations and baked him a cake. I nod politely but I don't really understand.

Some time later – years? months? – I trip over the Holocaust in a book I picked up somewhere. I read, aghast. *Surely* this never happened? Much later on at school, we are shown a film about the liberation of Belsen. I don't know if they still do this at schools now, but I think they should. My mother has to sit with me for hours at night time, trying her best to explain things to me. It is the first time that even the concept of evil has encroached in my world. I am inconsolable, and have many sleepless nights and terrible nightmares.

Rationing is over but I have inherited my mother's fear of waste. I am constantly imploring people not to leave anything and gathering up stale bits of bread to make bread puddings that nobody really wants to eat. Have you ever *seen* the rations that they had in WWII laid out on a table? The amount of butter my mother had in one week is probably what I'd spread on one piece of hot toast. I fret about food waste and am mortified if so much as a bag of salad slips past its best by date in my fridge. It seems shameful when half the world is starving. Even as a child I hated seeing food fights: an extravagant waste that angers far more than it amuses. I recently read about a diet that implores you to just half of what is on your plate. Leave *half*? Leave anything?!

In 1962 I see the film of Mutiny on the Bounty and have the satisfaction of knowing Captain Bligh (Trevor Howard) still owes my mother a pint of Guinness. At least.

Chapter 6

Thunder Tea

Thunder Tea

Strong Assam Tea

A fine single malt (preferably from the lowlands – nothing too peaty). Add the whisky to the tea and serve in a bone china cup and saucer.

I am sitting on Grace Helen's bed wrapping Christmas presents. I am not very adept at it but then neither is she. Her excuse is a severe stroke. Mine is that I am an impatient, cack-handed nine-year-old. We have more Sellotape around us than on the wrapping paper. The Christmas tree, topped with star and replete with delicate, glittering blown glass ornaments harking back to pre-war Austria, is in Grace Helen's room. This was a dining room but is now her bedroom. She is sipping Thunder Tea. It's something that adults only drink at Christmas, tea with a slug of whisky in it. It smells *awful*.

We reel off the litany of who is coming for Christmas. The Aunts, of course. Ruth, Ella *and* Margaret, who now lives in Canada where she has discovered a long lost daughter who is about my mother's age. At least, that's how it's put to me. Years later that I realise an illegitimate daughter wasn't easily accounted for then. Although it puzzled me how a mother could actually *lose* a daughter so I kept a very careful eye on my mother when we were out together. This daughter, Patricia, has a son, Andrew, who is about my age. He is coming too. I'm not wildly excited by this. Boys, in my village school experience, are often a disappointment. (What changes?) They play incomprehensible games, ride bikes around and like to show off scabby knees with a swaggering pride. Horrid.

'Who else?' I demand.

'Your Uncle John and Jessie, the *miserable* woman, and of course Uncle Michael and Dorothy, the idolater, and Freddy, of course.'

'What's an idolater?'

'Never you mind, it's a bit like a papist.'

Religion again, I sighed. I'd been Arch Angel Gabriel in the school Christmas play and, apart from the thrill of wearing a large pair of glitzy wings, it hadn't moved me in any way. I had rather hoped the Lord would make his presence felt with some sort of miracle but nothing much had happened, apart from Simon Duckworth tripping over his robes (he had an exacting part of one of the three kings and was weighed down with a massive gold turban and fake beard which made his stumble understandable but I had a sneaky suspicion he would have done it anyway, being a *boy*).

'Where are they all going to *sleep*?' I demand, already knowing I will have to surrender my bedroom.

'In rows like sardines on the front lawn,' Grace Helen says tartly.

My mother comes in with some hot chestnuts that have been baked in the oven, their tops snipped off, for us to shell. I fling myself across the bed so that she doesn't see her present that I am wrapping. It is some face cream from Helena Rubenstein that I have chosen myself torturously saving pocket money for *weeks*. It is pink frosted glass with a gold top, and is possibly the most sophisticated thing in the world.

More chestnuts go into our mouths than into the bowl. I glance out of the window, praying for snow. I plead with Grace Helen to have a word with the Almighty, with whom she seems to have a very reliable relationship. A bit like a woman with her dressmaker. You know *you're* paying her, but *she* really has all the power. Grace Helen says she'll do what she can but it's a very busy time of year.

My mother swoops down on the chestnuts before we polish them off and I follow her into the kitchen to help make the stuffing. The turkey has been plucked and sits hunched and naked on the kitchen table.

A plywood box of tangerines is on the floor, the fruits wrapped in tissue with an occasional tinsel flower dotted amongst them. Tangerines only ever arrive at Christmas and seem like a breath of orange flame in the gloomy English winter. Dates, too. I don't like the cloying dull taste of them but I am in love with the packaging and who wouldn't be? Palm trees and a caravanserai of camels trekking through sand dunes under a clear midnight sky sparkling with stars.

Christmas wouldn't be Christmas without them and certain other festive foods: crystallised fruits, preserved ginger, fruit cake, plum pudding (with the danger of breaking a tooth on the buried silver coin within), brandy butter, Stilton cheese, celery and pineapples (till the advent of tinned pineapple blew 'the only for Christmas' rule). Oh, and after all that, a tin of Andrews Liver Salts.

I stir the stuffing with a giant wooden spoon watching my mother chop dark green curly parsley and soak up the spirit of Christmas and all the delicious special smells.

Can anything beat the excitement of Christmas as a child?

Soon, I am lost in the influx of relations and friends arriving for our Christmas Eve party. I am kissed so much that I think it will permanently mark me. My cheeks *hurt* with all the kisses being planted. Among the crowd is Andrew, the boy cousin from Canada.

My first thought is – he looks mad.

He has white blond hair and staring pale blue eyes. He looks angelic but creepy. I am meant to 'get on' with him and show him around. Of course, I do no such thing and cling obstinately to my mother or my Uncles or Aunts. Anyone but him. Andrew and I eye each other with mistrust.

We're soon sent to bed and later that night he wakes me to open the stockings Father Christmas has filled. I take great delight in telling him that it was my mother, not Santa. His eyes brim with tears and I am struck speechless by this wimpish behaviour. What a *baby*.

He then tells anyone who'll listen that I am ruining his Christmas. He kicks me under the table and pinches Marmaduke, who gives a warning growl causing my father to banish him to the garden. Andrew smirks and I give him my best withering glance. He steals one of my presents, pretending it's for him, and then cheats at hats. I am *not* happy.

Lunch is, as usual, a glorious feast but it is marred by the revolting sight of Andrew eating like a toddler with his mouth open. We all sway at our chairs like sated pythons.

Presents are ripped apart, nuts are cracked and port sipped but all the time I am aware that Andrew is waiting for an opportune moment to somehow get me.

So I decide to get him first.

I take him outside and gently, but firmly, tell him that he is not really part of the family. After all, he must have noticed that he looks so different from the rest of us. He is, I tell him, only here on *approval* (a phrase I've heard Grace Helen and my mother say grandly on the phone when ordering something from a posh shop) and that I, and I alone, have been given the power to decide whether he stays in England or gets returned to Canada by himself where he will be sent straight away to an *orphanage*. He stares wide-eyed at me. I warm to the theme of the orphanage where tiny frozen boys huddle under moth eaten blankets, fighting to gnaw on the one crust of bread they are given. Their heads are shaved and they have to do really, *really* hard maths lessons for at least five hours every day.

'Are there rats?'

'Oh yes. Loads.'

He tells me that his mother would never allow this to happen. I reason with him that she is not his real mother and she has no choice in the matter. Only I do.

I gloat for the rest of the day and Andrew is beyond nice to me.

This behaviour is, of course, observed by my mother and

Grace Helen. The game is finally up when Andrew has nightmares and wets the bed.

My rules, *my* house, *my* family. That's my feeble and, it has to be said, flawed argument.

'How could you be so cruel?' my mother keeps asking me.

I shrug.

I have the same reaction years later when a friend pinches a chip from my plate. I have to restrain myself from stabbing her hand with my fork. It's *mine*. Get your own. The threat of a thieving outsider. Surely a primitive fear deep within us all.

Some of us handle it better than others.

Years later, the Lord does make an appearance and Andrew hears Him telling him that he must go and sift for gold in the swamps of Saskatchewan. He's probably still there. Raising funds for orphans.

Chapter 7

Abroad

Aioli

*5 peeled cloves of fresh garlic
1 dessertspoon of fresh breadcrumbs
1 large free range egg yolk
Dollop of Dijon mustard
salt and pepper
half a pint of extra virgin olive oil (or half sunflower oil)*

In a pestle and mortar cream the garlic, salt, pepper and breadcrumbs to a smooth paste. Scrape into a bowl. Add the egg yolk, mustard and a drop of the oil. Beating with a whisk, add the rest of the oil drop-by-wrist-breaking-drop, then slowly in a stream as it begins to thicken. Gather a selection of raw young vegetables – radish, turnip, broad beans, tiny boiled new potatoes, endive, chicory – and hard boiled eggs and dip in.

Holidays, up till now, have been in Cornwall or Brittany. Clotted cream, scones and great brown crabs make up the memories of the English Riviera. Sand between the toes and *bracing* walks. Garlic, crêpes and fish soup and yet *more* bracing walks are the memories of northern France. But then, one year, it is decided we are going to the *South* of France. It is the year that Grace Helen dies. It is felt that a month in the sun is called for.

I don't mind too much about Grace Helen. She has been very ill and I can see that she wants to leave this world. She visits me for weeks after she dies, sitting on a chair in my bedroom, tapping her walking stick against the foot of my bed. I don't tell anyone about these nocturnal visits, not even my mother. I sense that it would somehow send her over the edge. She is in a place that I cannot reach.

Devastated by grief over her mother, another tragedy hits. Michael dies too. He is very young (although 37 seems old to me as all adults tend to look the same age). The whole family is reeling with anguish tinged with hysteria. Things happen so quickly I can't keep up. Grace Helen is buried in a cemetery that has broken stone angels standing guard over the granite gravestones. We go there often with picnics and flowers. Michael is buried at sea and, as is usual in our family, the funeral quickly becomes a farce. At sea.

The captain of the hired boat is drunk, bad weather springs up out of nowhere and the boat hurls itself around the rough sea like a plastic duck in an emptying bath. Dorothy has placed a bottle of whisky, Michael's gun and his five year diary in his coffin. My mother decides that she wants the diary. My aunt is horrified and refuses. My father intervenes. A scene develops with my mother and my aunt, fighting seasickness and one another in a ladylike grapple over the coffin. A screwdriver is produced and, oh god, the coffin is opened. The captain obligingly starts to head the boat – according to my father – towards the Cape of Good Hope.

The Vicar throws up over the side of the boat, losing the top set of his false teeth. The wreaths, that were going to be placed lovingly on the forgiving bosom of the sea, fly off the deck and, in the strong wind, promptly boomerang back hitting John over the head.

'Michael, you swine! You're enjoying all this aren't you?' he shouts, shaking his fist at the heavens, towards his dead brother. Mingled tears of laughter and sorrow convulse us all.

Another boat, seeing the concentric circles we are making in the heavy swell, signals to see if we are in distress.

Yes, I rather think we are.

Even I can see that a month in the sun is most definitely called for.

We leave Marmaduke with Freddy, who looks nervous at this responsibility and wrings his hands at our departure. We offer to take him with us but he refuses, claiming he is too old now for foreign travel. The loss of his card partner has hit him hard and he looks, for the first time to me, an *old* man. As we leave, I see Marmaduke sitting on Freddy's silk upholstered armchair, looking smug. My father remarks that by the time we get back Marmaduke will have manicured paws or that Freddy will have taken up wearing tweeds. My mother bets on the former.

The car is bursting with clothes, books, papers, tea, gin, tennis rackets, pillows, and tins of Germolene. There is very little room for me in the back seat and I have to curl myself around hard, lumpy objects. I ask, just as we leave the end of our road, if we are nearly there yet. I continue asking at regular intervals. I drive *myself* mad, never mind my parents, who have that stoic look of people who know they're in for a long haul.

The drive takes days. Literally. I view most of northern France upside down, lying on the back seat. Endless rows of poplars streak by. As a child time passes fast or seemingly not at all depending on what you're doing. A maths lesson can last for *hours*. A picnic – minutes. We stop overnight at strange *pensions* that smell faintly of drains and garlic where I still feel as though I am in the car and hear traffic in my head. We have steak one night and my mother says she thinks it's horse. I assume she's joking. Then I find out. I am *horrified*. Maybe Abroad isn't going to suit me at all if they eat Black Beauty? We clean our teeth in bottled water and amongst the lumpy pillows I dream of Grace Helen.

One day in the car I am aware something different is happening outside the windows. It is my first glimpse of a southern sky and light. I take to it immediately as all creatures born in the cold grey north do. Pine woods have gone to be replaced with, what are they? *Olive groves*. It seems deeply exotic. I make up my mind there and then that I am going to *love* olives. And I do. Every goat I see, I point out in amazement, till it gets tedious. Eventually, we arrive.

I think the villa is a friend of a friend's. My parents stayed here before I was born, which I get rather huffy about. (How dare they have a life before *me*?) As soon as we leave the stuffy car we are plunged into the scented air of the region: thyme, resin, sun baked stone. The villa is a delight. Whitewashed, with the faded blue shutters that I have seen in the village nearby, it stands on the top of a hill made of terraces. These terraces are roughly paved with stones welded together with weeds and thistles. Only just level enough to balance a table and chairs on. Inside, it is cool with deep red smooth tiles on the floor and sparse, light furniture. The bathroom doesn't have a loo! A tiled hole set in the floor with footprints marked for standing or squatting shocks me to my core. Again, I am beset with worries about being *Abroad*.

I should be worrying about my parents. They are too quiet. Then they're snapping at one another. My father doesn't smile at *all*. Something is wrong. But what? I start to suck my thumb, something I haven't done since I was about four. This enrages my father who shouts at me every time he sees me do it so I take to hiding in corners.

I sense that all is not right but I don't know what to do. As in all situations that leave me feeling anxious – I eat. There is an abundance of fruit and I gorge myself on it. Apricots, green almonds, figs, perfumed melons, grapes, peaches and strawberries are all squashed into my mouth. My mouth and fingers are stained with juice. Subsequently I spend a lot of time squatting over the tiled hole in the floor wishing I was at home in our bathroom with its lovely loo.

One morning I awake to hear the car moving away. I lean out of the window and see my father driving down the hill. I assume he has gone into the village to buy the delicious bread and croissants we all love for breakfast. I turn over and doze, planning what to do that day. Maybe the beach then a long swim in the warm sea? I wake up, much later, to find my mother in a *rage*. She tells me that my father has left us. For good. For ever. He is *not* coming back.

This seems not only improbable but impossible.

I look around the villa and see broken glasses and smashed plates. When did this happen? Why didn't I hear it? *What is going on?*

My mother, with shaking hands, pours a gin and tonic for herself and passes me one too. She is not upset, she is *furious*. I have only ever seen her like this a few times before and it is terrifying. Her blue eyes flash like steel as she paces the villa hitting out at any piece of furniture that gets in her way. Suddenly she picks up an empty wine bottle and hurls it, with great violence, against the wall. I duck as shattered splinters of glass spray the room then crouch in the corner, crying silently. She picks up a heavy cast iron saucepan and starts pounding it against the floor, cracking the tiles. She looks quite demented. I remember the story of Mrs Tiggywinkle – the hedgehog that reverts back to the wild. I am frozen in panic at the sight of my mother becoming a wild animal.

I don't know what to do. *I don't know what to do.*

My mother is a feral cat, her fury reverberating around the room. She could well grow claws and hiss. She suddenly stops, perhaps exhausted by her efforts, and sees me, as if for the first time. Immediately she holds out her arms and I run to her. We spend a long time standing in the room of that rented villa, tightly holding one another.

That evening we walk into the village and my mother makes mysterious phone calls from a public phone in a café. We order lobster and eat it with our fingers. We order wine, and I don't have it diluted with water. We walk back up the hill arm in arm. I half expect to see the car back there, but it's not.

That night I sleep in her bed.

The following day, Uncle John arrives in a big black car. As soon as he walks in, looking hot and tired, I know then that it's true. My father is really never coming back. My parents are going to be *divorced*.

We spend a few more days at the villa. We go to the markets and I glimpse another way of life. I taste unheard of delights, salami, goat's cheese, ratatouille, crème a la Coeur and cassis. On the last day, my mother and my uncle make that eternal mayonnaise – aioli. We eat it outside and I gaze at the Mediterranean landscape already aware that it will always remind me of the day I became fatherless. I turn the word over in my head, tasting it.

My mother and John make so much noise, that all the goats in the olive grove come to investigate. Brother and sister sit in the sunshine planning their lives without my father. They are talking and laughing and vying with one another to chase the bad stuff away. They are subtly, and not so subtly, trying to make me feel that everything will somehow be *all right*. It's true that my father has many unattractive habits, though he did let me sit on his lap when the daleks crossed London Bridge. He inclines towards the morose, likes sports and makes me join in things that, frankly, I abhor (I am so much happier with my nose in a book than chasing a ball). He doesn't like having the house full of people, buys new shoes and *smells* them, and didn't find it funny that I bought him the Johnny Cash record 'A boy named Sue' for Christmas. He's inflexible. The list goes on. Is it long enough? Long enough to enable me to laugh at him, and not feel sorry that he's gone? I try my best. I desperately want my mother not to be unhappy, but most of all I don't want to have to deal with her fury again.

It is hot. I am sleepy with garlic and wine. As I doze in the shade of a tree I overhear my mother tell John that she will have The Trout's guts for garters, that my father can plead on bended knee but that she will never relent. I hear John give a deep sigh and tell her that he, too, has left his wife (the miserable Jessie) and will move in with us. He also tells her that he has joined something called the AA. I don't understand this because I know we belong to the RAC. Is it the same thing? Why is joining a club with something to do with cars said in such an important sounding voice? But I am delighted about my uncle living with us.

We are spared the gruelling drive home by John booking seats on a plane. My mother hates flying and, closing her eyes, clutches my hand throughout the flight. When we land in England she says at the top of her voice: 'Dear God, the engines have stopped!' We reassure her that's because we have landed and then, and only then, does she do something very untypical. She cries.

In times of need, I feed. I know it's not terribly romantic. I wonder what it would be like to be one of those waif-like creatures who, in times of emergency, must be plied with morsels by anxious friends imploring them to 'eat something, anything, just to keep your strength up'. Oh no, not me. At the slightest sign of stress or first twinge of pain, I am foraging in the kitchen.

I never saw my father again. And now I expect all men to behave like him. And, *of course*, because I expect it, they do. I smugly sit back waiting for him to leave so I can prove myself right. Next time, I'll do it *differently*, I promise. I don't.

Alcohol was used in our family to enhance things. Fallen in love with a husky stranger? Tell all over a glass of wine. Good day at work? Let's toast it with champagne! It's no wonder I struggle with the concept of *enough* of anything. Enough sounds mean spirited. If one cocktail is good, surely two is better? Even when I am having an utterly fantastic time, I find myself unconsciously searching for the thing that will improve it, make it bigger or better. Alcohol, chemicals, cigarettes—they all work. But it's the cupboards I come back to.

Chapter 8

Dinner Lady's Surprise

No recipe (mercifully)

The village primary school is a torment to me. Vast classes run by mad adults – or so it seems. I manage to carve out a niche for myself by sitting at the back of the room and keeping my nose firmly in a book. Miss Conant, the small, iron haired woman who scares us all, singles me out for unwanted attention. I know she hates me. Why? I'm not sure. She instructs me to mime during singing lessons. Fair enough – I am spectacularly tone deaf but so is every one else. Well, they are to me, anyway. She makes me stand up and do convoluted 'mental arithmetic' in front of the whole class. If it takes seven men five days to build three miles of rail track how long would it take five men? Who knows? Who cares? Supposing one of them gets ill? What if a cow wanders on to the track? Too many variables and a sense of deep indifference leave me speechless and unable to comply. Miss Conant makes scathing comments about me and the whole class sycophantly giggles. I *loathe* her. I start to have nightmares and dread going to school.

My only respite is that I am allowed home for lunch.

Sometimes I don't go back – Strawy is easily swayed into believing that I have headaches. We spend afternoons reading in the garden or huddled in front of a fire making toast. All this changes after my father leaves and Grace Helen is no longer around. My mother gets a job and I *have* to stay at school for lunch.

Dear *God*, the food that we are given is truly terrible. There are no kitchens in the school and the meals arrive in the back of a van. You can smell it coming up the road. You'd have to be wearing a gas mask to avoid it. Massive trays of glistening white undercooked pastry covering what smells like tinned dog food. Vats of lumpy mash, tin jugs of watery gravy and acres of soggy cabbage. My heart sinks. I know I won't be able to eat this. But then, I reason with a triumphant surge of gladness, *nobody* will.

I take my place in the queue and hear the chants of, 'small, please Mrs Welch'. Mrs Welch is one of the white clad dinner ladies who doles out the pie. We are allowed to say small or large (as if!) and to refuse gravy. I nervously clutch my plate and ask for small of everything, shudder at the gravy poured, or dug out – depending on the amount of flour that has been dumped in it by a prefect (a job I somehow know I'll never attain). I then have to go to a different serving table for pudding. It is semolina, or so I assume, having never seen this particular form before. Slopped out by yet another responsible prefect and enlivened by a dollop of unnaturally bright red jam, it appears to be made of wood pulp. I place the two plates in front of me and stare in horror.

I glance around and see other children piling things into

their mouths. Perhaps it's like being in Paris? Maybe it's not as bad as it looks? I nervously cut a minute piece of pie and gingerly put it in my mouth. My back teeth spring open as I hit a bit of gristle. I feel sick. I push my plate to one side and gaze at everyone else in wonderment. Perhaps they've all got different taste buds to me? I manoeuvre the lump of gristle into my hand and discreetly drop it on the floor. The two girls either side of me condescendingly explain that I have to have clear both plates. I am not allowed to leave anything.

I stare at them.

They stare back.

I watch other children carrying their plates up to a teacher (*oh god*, it's Miss Conant) showing off their empty plates before dropping their bent tin cutlery (do they think we're all going to slash our wrists if they give us proper knives?) into a plastic bucket and stacking their plates into an ever growing pile.

I am stunned.

I have never before been made to eat anything I didn't like. It strikes me (and still does) as an act of cruelty.

I know that I can't eat this. My throat is closing up at the very thought of it. The two girls look pityingly at me, and tell me that it's not that bad.

Are they *insane*?

Nearly all the children have managed the pie and are stirring the jam into the sludge of the semolina.

Later, I learn that this is the worst of the puddings. Apparently they make one called gypsy tart, which is popular because of the rhyme that goes with it:

Gypsy tart
makes you fart.
Custard powder
makes it louder!

I sit staring at my rapidly cooling plates. I glance over at Miss Conant and see a smile spread over her face. This strengthens my resolve to sit it out. I am, after all, the high priestess of the cold stare. I have practised it in the past on various arch enemies and always win. It helps that I have bright green eyes, and am, though I don't yet know, very short sighted.

Half an hour later I am the only person left in the tin hut they call the canteen.

The battle rages.

Miss Conant is near retirement age and has her grey hair in earphones (the only hairstyle that has never come back into fashion unless you count Princess Leah in Star Wars). She tries every trick on the book: shouting, sarcasm, intimidation and bullying.

I am impervious, making a deal with myself that I will only succumb to tears when I am back *home*. (This is quite a handy trick to learn and has served me in good stead over the years.)

Mrs Welch and the rest of the dinner ladies are wiping down tables and taking off their hairnets, getting ready to leave. They natter amiably amongst themselves, ignoring me, while they turn themselves back into ordinary middle aged women. I give them pleading stares but they continue to chat with the dreaded Miss Conant. It makes me understand how guards in prisons can obey orders. As soon as they leave, Miss Conant swoops down on me and tries to force a forkful of pie between my closed lips. I bite her. She slaps me. I start screaming.

All hell breaks loose.

The headmaster, a portly man with the unlikely name of Mr Clutterbuck that we must address as 'Sir', hoves into view. My mother is telephoned and summonsed from work. The minute I see Strawy I know everything will be all right. She is unquestionably on my side. She is horrified that I am being force fed. I am taken home and given strawberries and cream. I beg Strawy to be allowed to come home for lunch, as I did in the past. She spends the evening explaining to me that it is impossible. I try my hardest to be grown up about it but the harsh financial realities of adult life are hard for me to grasp.

My mother makes me a salty egg and watercress sandwich to take to school next day and pushes in an apple and a slice of fruit bread into a plastic box but I still have to go to the canteen.

The following day I invent something called dinner lady's surprise. It involves scraping everything from your lunch plate onto your pudding plate, squishing the lot down firmly then putting the empty, so called 'clean' plate on top, thereby being able to present a clean plate to the attending teacher. It is taken up by all and sundry. Miss Conant wears a bandage on her hand for a long time but leaves me alone.

I decide that I despise school.

Strawy sympathises but is unable to help. She makes up for it by preparing delicious food at home, even going so far as heroically buying 'packet' food which is the height of fashion. Vesta Chow Mein is the favoured thing. It is like space food and comes in sealed foil packages that have to be re-hydrated. It even has a tiny individual packet of soya sauce. I imagine I'm exploring distant galaxies in a rocket and plead for it at least once a week.

I go from being a bookish, quiet girl to being utterly obnoxious. I discover that teachers don't really have any power. I get away with murder. There are mutterings, that I am only just aware of, of a 'troubled home life'. It seems incredible now, but I think I really was the only child in my school whose parents were getting divorced. It was unheard of.

School food. Hating it is elementary. We all remember hideous dishes of boiled grey horror and glaucous mystery meats in scary sauces.

Somehow I get in to grammar school where I am deemed 'out of control'. Strawy sends me to a 'free thinking' co-ed boarding school in the west country. This is meant to re-awaken my interest in education but all it does is underscore my belief that there is a good case for letting some children leave school at the age of about eleven. The head master *there* (do call me Graham) has a thing about fish. A big thing. I think he'd spent some time in Japan and we had it, raw, at nearly every meal. Including breakfast. This was long time before the first sushi bar hit Britain and we all despaired at the oily slabs of cold mackerel that were oh so good for us. We were all so hungry, all of the time, that my boyfriend, Laurie, and I devised a plan.

We began buying the local paper which gave notices of

weddings. Every Saturday we would put on our best clothes – it was the early Seventies so the clothes, frankly, were never 'best' but we did what we could with platform heels, purple velvet loon pants, a smelly grubby Afghan coat and a variety of kipper ties and floral shirts. We'd set off to the church on Laurie's scooter. Arriving we would confidently claim to be with the bride's party (guessing, quite rightly as it turned out, that the bride *always* had more guests than the groom). After lustily singing all the hymns and beaming encouragingly at the be-meringued bride we'd follow on to the reception and devour plate after plate, stuffing what we couldn't eat into bags and pockets for later.

No one ever questioned us. Now I find this improbable, especially as Laurie was West Indian with a huge Afro – not an every day sight in rural Devon. There must be countless wedding photographs where couples still ask themselves who the hell was that couple standing at the back looking like something from Hair? Now you know. Sorry.

What children eat now worries me. I know the harried and hurried working mother can't always rustle up a delicious home cooked meal but what are we doing to our children? Fast food is fast killing them and their taste buds. Thank God for Jamie Oliver. Really.

Certain foods will always be loathed – barely tolerated by adults, let alone children (who have far more sensitive palates). A bad taste to a child is *mountainous not merely momentary.* Imagine a ten foot policewoman trying to make you eat beetroot or offal or cold rice pudding or whatever. Let's encourage children to try different food but, please, let's not force them.

I am no longer a child but to this day I couldn't, for anything or anyone, eat: tripe, Swiss chard, margarine, liver, marzipan, mashed swede, halva or a hot dog. Or semolina.

Chapter 9

Sickie Blanket

Steak and Kidney Pudding

This really is a dish fit for kings. Or Uncles.

2 lbs chuck steak (or skirt)
1/2 lb ox kidney
1 onion
Handful of chopped mixed herbs
Salt and pepper
Seasoned flour
1 lb suet crust

Now, I know that suet seems a really horrible thing, but it isn't. Honestly. All you need to do is mix 1/2 lb of flour with about 5 oz of suet with cold water till it forms a dough. That's it. Chop the meat, kidney and onion in small pieces. Line a well greased 8 inch pudding bowl with two-thirds of the suet dough. Roll the meat in the seasoned flour and add to the bowl with the onion and herbs. Season well. Pour in enough cold water to fill the bowl to about two-thirds. Squidge out the remaining dough to form a lid, press down firmly on the sides and then swaddle the whole thing in a clean tea towel and immerse in a saucepan of boiling water for about 4 hours. Top up with boiling water now and then, if the pan runs dry.

Take to the table in a clean cloth with a jug of boiling water to augment the unctuous, glorious gravy inside the pudding.

I would serve this with mash and buttered peppered cabbage but I am very big on carbs.

Darling Uncle John, complete with his tickling moustache and hands that smell of smoked bacon due to his excessive cigar habit, comes to live with us. Strawy and I are delighted. We have spent three days shunting furniture around the house. Grace Helen's room reverts back into a dining room, the best spare bedroom has a coat of paint slapped on it and the breakfast room is stripped of its tat and junk to make way for a desk and chair.

Strawy hates decorating so to make the job more interesting she's wearing her wedding dress. The split and faded white train dips in and out of the paint and I am allowed to wear the veil, even though it impedes my vision meaning a lot more paint gets spilt on the floor. No matter. We're happy. We don't have set meals; foraging in the fridge for odd little tit bits whenever we get hungry. My mother makes a jug of Pimms (mostly lemonade) to keep us going and we sip through straws the scent of cucumber and paint fumes.

I demand to be told more about her wedding day which somehow isn't connected to my father, whom we rarely speak of now. I instinctively get, that for most women the Big Day is about the day itself, not the man. *He* might as well be a cardboard cut out.

'Well, let me think. Grace Helen cried in the morning because she had always wanted to wake me up with tray of tea and champagne, entering a room that had flowers and sun streaming through the windows. She did manage the champagne and tea but she had to wear gum shoes because we were in the bomb shelter. Goodness it was damp. Papa had it built in the back of the garden: mud everywhere, the roof dripped, sandbags for walls, *not* the most romantic setting. When we got to the church there was a terrible dog fight going on overhead and all through the service you could hear gunfire and engines ... dreadful noise, poor souls. Of course the honeymoon, which was meant to be Venice but was in fact Dublin, was appalling, though the food was lovely. Roast goose. Very nice. Grace Helen adored your father, which made it all the more difficult about Stewart of course.'

I nod, diffidently. I have heard of Stewart before but I am a bit hazy on the details. I have a stuffed toy dog called Freckles that has a silver tag around his neck which I know once belonged to him. It has a musty smell and in places the fur has been worn away. Freckles has very fetching amber glass eyes held in by steel pins that can be removed for extra comic effect. Both my parents knew Stewart but I have never met him or, if I have, I can't remember. I decide that now is the time to press for details.

My mother wipes her hands down her paint streaked wedding dress.

'Oh Stewart, well, he was a *lovely* man,' she says warmly, 'Very unusual colouring, that's what I saw first. Freckles and that really *dark* red hair. Tall, well, so was your father of course, but Stewart, well . . . and his voice, goodness it was velvety, and his laugh . . .' she sighs, and looks critically at the skirting board which is patchy with undercoat.

I nudge her. She continues.

'Well, it was all very difficult, although we did manage it rather well. Your father and he became very good friends, that's why we all lived together, of course, it made sense, what with the rations and everything,' she adds vaguely.

This hits me with a jolt. They all *lived* together? What did she do, take it in turns to sleep with them? Maybe they all slept together? No, *surely* not. I am just discovering sex. Not actual sex but the idea of it. The mechanics of it all seem incomprehensible and a bit scary but the romance is thrilling.

'A cottage in the country, no, you've never seen it. A German parachutist came down in the back garden, we gave him tea before the police arrived. He wouldn't drink it, I expect he thought it was poisoned or something. Fool. Not an English thing to do at all. I can't think of any famous English poisoners, can you? Apart from Sweeney Todd or did he just murder them and put them in pies? Anyway, it was all going terribly well, and for some unaccountable reason your father put his foot down about it. Made me choose.'

I gaze round eyed at her. Strawy is all things to me, the centre of my world in fact, but I had never seen her before as a romantic heroine. Having to choose between men strikes me as the sort of thing that film stars do, not mothers. Certainly not *my* mother. It also strikes me that this is *not* like meanderings of a memsahb. She is not making this up.

'I went to Scotland to stay with friends and think about it. They both met me when I returned at Kings Cross station and that's when I decided. Stewart was holding the most *enormous* bouquet of hot house flowers, terribly hard to get during the war, you know. Your father had a badly battered bunch of daffodils done up in newspaper. I felt so terribly sorry for him, you see. We all went for dinner and your father was very nice about the whole thing. It was decided that Stewart and I should go away together, a sort of long goodbye holiday. The war had just ended and – can you believe it – Stewart won the football pools! So, he bought a car, oh, it was lovely, it had belonged to the Prince of Wales, and we won the concourse d'elegance in it in the South of France. I was mistaken for Tallulah Bankhead of all people. Hmm? Yes, I went back to your father, as agreed. No I never saw Stewart again.'

I insist on finding out what happened to Stewart even though I sense I am not going to like what I hear. I can hear her voice slowly becoming softer, sadder.

'Stewart? Well, he went back to Ireland. I had a telegram from him saying that he was catching the ferry to Liverpool, and would I meet him. This was a year or so later. I knew I had to, it had been a mistake choosing your father. I blame the bloody daffs, never liked them since. So I jumped on a train and went to Liverpool.'

'And?' I prompt, spellbound.

'Stewart never caught the ferry. He was killed driving that beautiful car to the port.'

I pour my mother another glass of Pimms and cuddle her. It's not much but it's all I can do.

We finish painting the walls of what is to be Uncle John's bedroom and survey them with pride. It crosses my mind that Uncle John might not like flamingo pink. Strawy adds her own particular brand of creativity to it by splashing the walls with gold paint. Let's just say the working girls of the *vieux* port of Marseille would feel at home.

When Uncle John arrives he immediately praises the room, wiping away tears of laughter. His presence in the house is tangible. Gone are the fairy like, make shift snacks and back come regular hearty meals. To celebrate his arrival, my mother makes his favourite supper (steak and kidney pudding) and we invite Freddy and other friends to join us.

Other things change too. The drinks cupboard is emptied. I don't quite see the significance of this, though I do see Uncle John searching through it one morning with shaking hands.

John and Strawy take up oil painting and arrange easels in the shabby book lined room that we jokingly call the library. Screams of laughter echo round the house as they compare work. My mother thinks that portraiture is her forte but will only paint left side profiles and won't attempt hands at all. She has also invested in a stack of pre-cut small canvases. These make them all look like Ruritanian midgets with a genetic flaw that renders them handless, posing for a new coin or stamp. John favours still life. Plates of fruit and great jugs of wilting flowers arranged in Cézanne-like piles are hazards to avoid on the way to the bathroom during the night.

We still have parties and he still makes everyone laugh but he now holds a glass of orange juice or ginger ale in his hands while pouring cocktails for everyone else.

His divorce and my mother's are running parallel and I soon add a whole new lexicon of words to my grown up vocabulary: adultery, maintenance, due cause, alimony and mortgages are just a few. Others include bastard, bitch and swindler.

I don't have to be told that finances are perilous.

New shoes are a thing of the past and when I feel my toes being cramped into my old winter boots I try not to say anything. It is, however, noticed that I am walking like a cripple.

We make a game of economies but it's hard. I don't really understand what's going on. Uncle John goes to London a lot but always comes home early, looking sad. I do my best to cheer him by sitting on his lap and pulling his moustache. He lets me play with his gold cufflinks till I accidentally swallow one. (Oh, the humiliation! I have to use a potty for *days*.)

The delivery men slowly stop coming to the house. In retrospect I think it was a combination of the general decline of such people as well as the gradual slowing down of orders from us.

One day I wake up and I can't swallow. I try to get out of bed and fall on the floor. I am *delighted*. I am ILL. That means – no school. Strawy leaves Uncle John in charge of me and we have a delightful morning baking a cake. John is a very good cook but he's no baker and weighs and measures all the ingredients with a scowl of concentration and a constant flow of chatter.

'Four ounces, bloody silly, let's make it five, shall we? Now then, it says here we need the grated rind of an orange.

Have we got one? No, I thought not, well, a lemon will have to do. Now then, are you feeling up to measuring out some milk? Good girl. Brown sugar. Hmm, *brown*, well, that's a bit of a challenge, isn't it? What about golden syrup? I'd call that brown, wouldn't you?'

The last thing I remember is seeing the sticky flow of syrup from the enchanting green tin with the lion and a swarm of bees on it.

I wake up in hospital.

All thoughts of missing school have been replaced with the conviction that I am about to die. Nobody seems to know what is wrong with me. Some sort of throat, ear, head thing that manifests itself in terrifyingly high fevers and torrents of blood loss from my nose. Strawy tells me proudly that it took ages to clear the amount of blood from the kitchen floor. I demand to know how many pints.

'Oh. At least five,' she says comfortingly.

Uncle John says that the cake was divine and I ask for a slice.

I am incredulous when I'm told that the cake was made days and days ago. Where have I been all that time? It's explained that I have been lying in this hospital bed. No, I mean the *me* of me, where has that been? Drifting around the heavens talking to Grace Helen or communing with Uncle Michael or Ella? Or have I been plunged into a sort of coma waiting room where I have wafted about looking ill? I can't tell.

It is decided that I have to have an operation. *Now.* A sort of tonsillectomy/abscess removal and general rootling around to see what's wrong. I am moved by ambulance to a teaching hospital in London. Barts. In the ambulance my mother keeps one hand firmly to her chest in a sort of heroic 'oh my god my poor daughter' pose. Hot blood pours again from my nose and I am screaming with agony by the time we arrive. The surgeon is waiting and I am wheeled into a theatre. I am used to being the centre of attention but even I am shaken into silence by the sheer drama of it all. Romantically, I consider making a last request but think that this might upset Strawy who has a look on her face that I have never seen before.

I later identify it: it's the look that we all have when someone we love is in pain and there is nothing we can do about it.

I am handed a small plastic glass of a vile tasting concoction and seconds after swallowing it have the delicious sensation of the ebbing away of pain and floating into clouds. Why was morphine not sold in my local sweet shop?

Recovery in Barts is pretty wonderful. The nurses are young girls who lark around and we have ice cream at every meal and I enjoy unlimited access to the library. The down side is that I have to use a bed pan. Dreadful memories of the cufflink swallowing incident assail me and I cannot 'go'. Strawy and John faithfully attend my every wish and soon I'm back home. I make Strawy recount again and again the ambulance ride and the operation. I don't mind that I am confined to my bed, indeed I rather relish it. The only thing I hate is the jigsaw puzzles I am given to do. These baffle and bore me and Strawy falls around laughing when she catches me filing a particularly difficult bit of blue sky down with a nail file to make it fit.

'*How* like Grace Helen!' she cries.

The traditional sickie blanket is placed reverently over my bed and I am thrilled with it, as it is only ever allowed over people *in extremis*. It is a patchwork, crotcheted affair, heavily fringed in wool. I twist and plait the fringes as I doze in and out of sleep.

I have invalid food, though how or why mashed banana is deemed to be suitable I don't know. But it is and I love it. The banana has to be squidged with a fork then tapped with the back of a teaspoon till it's glossy. Then – and only then – can a generous dose of cream be poured over it. Thin bread and butter is deemed a suitable accompaniment.

I am affronted when I am given homework to do. How dare they? Don't they know that I have been ILL? I am still to suffer the greater indignity of being visited by Miss Conant – I pretend to be asleep but don't think I fooled her. She leaves me a book about Hereward the Wake which I refuse to read.

Back at school I scare everyone with tales of the cruelty of hospitals and the agony of surgery. I ghoulishly recount how I nearly drowned in my *own blood*. I describe the operation in great detail (pure speculation, of course). How I had to be held down by three strong men, how the pain was so great and how the floor was *ankle deep* in scarlet gore. This is met with a suitably hushed awe. One poor girl is due to have her ears syringed and I traumatise her so much that she refuses to go to the surgery. She tells her parents that all doctors are the devil's pages who stick red hot pokers in your ears that burn you forever.

The best thing about the whole ordeal is that, henceforth,

I can pretty much get off school whenever I want to by clutching my throat.

Convalescence was a big thing when I was a child and I really wish it would make a comeback. Even the word – *convalescence* – has an Edwardian ring of comfort to it, conjuring up bath chairs heavily blanketed on a seaside veranda, maybe with a monkey puzzle tree in view. There was something really lovely about not being *quite* recovered enough to resume school yet not ill enough to be in bed. Special food and great books were encouraged. As were gentle occupations – nothing too strenuous, you understand. A week in a convalescent home sounds like my idea of a holiday. Perhaps I could open one?

Chapter 10

Everybody Must Get Stoned

Snape

I don't know why this was called snape in our household. I suppose it's just colcannon.

A simple, hearty, satisfying plate of mashed potato, with chopped spring onions that have been simmered in milk, butter and pepper which are added to the potatoes after they are mashed.

Curl up and enjoy – comforting beyond words.

My best friend is Michaela. She loathes grammar school too and we instantly unite in our common hatred. We hate *everything*. Our uniforms, the teachers, the rules, the games, the other girls, in fact we pretty much have a general hate fest going on about the whole hateful world. We are in our early teens and it's the early Seventies. We have easy access to excess.

We take liberties with our uniforms that make our mothers despair and our teachers put us in detention. We look as though we belong in some seedy men's magazine, the sort that isn't even on the top shelf but kept behind the counter so you have to know Spotty Sid to get at it. Our skirts are hiked up to *just* cover our bottoms. We wear dark tights with knee high white socks and platform shoes. Our shirts are tied beneath our just emerging bosoms and we loosely wear our school ties à la Frank Sinatra playing Vegas. We have smudgy eye make up and our hair is in heavy pre-Raphaelite waves (due to excessive spray and gel and obsessive grooming). Our mouths are kissable, if you could find them beneath dollops of crushed plum lipsticks and lip-gloss. We wear shades even in the winter and don't smile very much. Great look, huh? We are often mistaken for hookers. At least, I assume that what we're mistaken for as it's hard to tell through the shades and the eyeliner. Hookers with a penchant for literature. Because we also have, sticking out of pockets and bags, pretentious books by Simone de Beauvoir, Huysman, and any other rebel with or without a cause.

Michaela has the added advantage of being very tall and already enjoys a well formed bust. She has large brown eyes, long colt like legs and looks about eighteen. I am short, short sighted and seem to be enjoying a permanent bad hair day. She also seems to live with parents and a sister who genuinely don't care about where she goes or what she does. This seems amazing to me as Strawy is practically driven to a nervous breakdown with my appalling behaviour.

Adolescence (me) and the menopause (her) hit at the same time. Our home is hormone central.

Uncle John views me with amusement and tells Strawy not to worry. Ha! The woman was born to worry: Who are you going with/How are you getting home/Ten o'clock is late enough/I don't care what time Michaela has to be home and on it goes. Nag, nag, nag.

Being a nasty, hormone driven thirteen-year-old I think

she is being eminently unreasonable. On the plus side, she does do my homework for me. She adores geography and map tracing and we get away with it till the fateful day she leaves Germany out of a map of Europe. I am hauled to the front of the class and asked why Poland and Prague are slotted together. I peer at the map, puzzled. I manage to stammer out something about the treaty of Versailles and then we all look puzzled. Strawy also monkeys about with the counties of England, swapping Lancashire and Yorkshire. Needless to say I fail geography dismally.

In fact, I fail nearly every exam dismally.

I am too busy to do school work. Most of my time is taken up with Michaela. Our disenfranchised ranks have been swollen with Suzanne and Jackie. We spend every lunch hour sitting behind a bush (strictly out of bounds) at the end of the playing field talking about boys, music, and boys again while painting our nails and reading what we consider to be *underground* literature. We sneer at the girls who join the lacrosse team of their own free will and consider ourselves to be the Dorothy Parker set. The bush being our rough equivalent of the round table at the Algonquin. Others hover around our periphery but we ignore them. We have, of course, formed a cabal against the rest of the world. We try hard for the existentialist mood but often get sidelined by discussing what we'd do if Marc Bolan dropped by for a coffee.

Coffee is a *big* thing with us. There is an Italian café on the way home from school and we all congregate there sipping cappuccinos in a Milan meets Chislehurst sort of way. We sit scowling at the passers by, desperately hoping that we're creating the sort of café culture we so idealise.

This intense sophistication crumbles at the very proximity of any fanciable male as we revert to giggling imbeciles.

We also roll joints.

I am stoned for my entire secondary education. No wonder equations and fractions are still a mystery to me. Sometimes at weekends we go to Michaela's house and smoke ourselves into a paranoid hysteria. The conversation goes something like this.

'What do you wanna do tonight?'

'Dunno.'

'Nor me, but let's not go to the Black Prince.'

'No. They wouldn't serve me a bloody drink last week.'

'Fascists.'

'So, what do you wanna do?'

'Dunno.'

'Whatever we do, let's not go to the Black Prince, OK?'

'OK.'

'I hate the Black Prince, it's so like, *uncool*.'

'Yeah, me too.'

We stop this riveting dialogue to search for the dope. The fat, oily lump has rolled off the LP cover that we are skinning up on. The etiquette of smoking is that you *always* skin up on an LP cover. This time I think it's on Juicy Lucy which shows a naked woman writhing on a bed of fruit. Needless to say, the curtains are drawn against the sunlight and heavy music is pounding our ears. The pounding may well also be Michaela's father demanding we turn the volume down but she has a lock on her bedroom door so we ignore him. We smoke yet another joint and contemplate the evening's entertainment.

'So, what are we gonna do?'

'Dunno. What do you wanna do?'

'Well, I know what I *don't* wanna to do. I don't wanna go to the poxy Black Prince.'

'Nor me. Alo.'

'What do you really *really* wanna do. Alo.'

'Dunnoalo.'

'Fair enoughalo.'

We start to giggle helplessly at our Wildean wit and roll around the floor for a bit. I roll so much that I fall off the purple velvet bean bag that is the favoured mode of seating in Michaela's room. I drag myself upright and carefully lick the edges of some Rizla papers to make another joint. We have covered every eventuality of being this stoned and have thoughtfully provided ourselves with a munchie basket and pints of water. I reach into the basket and fish out a small pot of yoghurt.

'Damn. I hate hazelnut. Got any raspberry?'

'Nah. What's got a hazelnut in every bite?'

'Squirrel shit!'

Yet more yelps of helpless laughter force themselves from our bellies. The record finishes but we are too stoned to get up and change it, even though I have brought with me the new Led Zeppelin album that we really want to hear. But it's too much like hard work.

'What *are* we gonna do then?'

'I don't mind, really, but let's not go to the Black Prince, OK?'

'God, no, I wouldn't go there if they were giving away free dope.'

'Nor me.'

'Well, I wouldn't go there if they were giving away free money *and* dope.'

'No, nor me.'

I eventually summon the will to go home after arranging to meet Michaela and Suzanne at seven at the Black Prince.

That place is our Rome. All roads lead to it.

It is a huge, black and white fake Tudor bar/pub/concert hall. It is hideously ugly. It has, so they say, gone *down hill*. It serves practically anybody and on Thursday and Sunday nights it is hippie heaven. The loos smell, the floor is so sticky you have to keep moving or you will be rooted to the spot, it sells out of date peanuts and flat beer. All sorts of freaks hang out there. Bands, too. Our local bands play there regularly: Mott the Hoople, Status Quo, Medicine Head, Stray, they all congregate there. On a hot summer's evening you can smell the dope and patchouli oil before you can see the building. Cider and blackcurrant is the favoured drink, dope the drug *du jour*.

That evening I saunter towards the place, secure in the knowledge that Strawy is doing my homework (science, not geoggers – she longs to draw a Bunsen burner). I am wearing a long hand smocked dress that Strawy has lovingly made for me (despite pointing out that I look like a milk maid from Transylvania) and Grace Helen's ankle length black velvet opera coat. An armful of Indian bangles, black nail varnish, yellow knee length platform boots and a face full of slap complete the picture.

I see various other people drift by in haze of smoke and I am soon caught up in our loose network of friends. A rumour is going around that there is going to be a music festival on the Isle of Wight. Jimi Hendrix is going to play. *Jimi Hendrix*. It's a bit like the second coming. I am filled with longing. I *have* to go. I will never in a million light years be *allowed* to go, but I *have* to go.

Michaela and Suzanne come running towards me. So, they've heard it too. But, Michaela is smarter than me. She has A Plan.

The Plan is cunningly simple. Far too simple, as anyone but a stoned teenager would tell you. It consists of this. Suzanne will tell *her* mother that she is going to be staying with me and I will tell *my* mother that I am going to be staying with her. Dazzling, no?

Michaela doesn't have to bother with any of this. Her parents barely know that she attends school only occasionally.

We are stunned by the sheer brilliance of it. We start to plot how we are going to get there (a bloke called Bob has a van) and plan what we're going to wear. How we are going to actually *pay* for this trip to paradise is somewhat of a hurdle as collectively we can rustle up about three pounds fifty. We put this petty matter to one side and concentrate on the essentials.

'Can I borrow your crushed velvet dress? The long one that has the flared sleeves?'

'Only if I can borrow your Biba jacket.'

'We *must* get our ears pierced.'

'Do we need a tent?'

'Suppose so, and sleeping bags.'

I volunteer the information that we have those very things in the loft or lurking somewhere in the tumbledown garage and magnanimously offer to lend them out.

'Cool.'

'How are we gonna get them out of your place so that no one sees us?'

We ponder this for a while till Michaela says that we simply tell Strawy that we are going to take them over to Suzanne's and sleep out in the garden.

'Yeah, your mum's so cool that she'll probably make an apple pie or something for us.'

I have a twitch of guilt about this but brush it aside in that curious way only callous adolescents can. I adore Strawy but this is too big a deal for me to worry about hurting her. It is after all *Jimi Hendrix* that we are talking about here. It's as if Jesus were planning to speak at Cowes. We *have* to go.

Strawy is mystified. 'But you hate camping, do you remember when we went to the New Forest and you wanted to know where the carpet was? And you said that you were never going over to Suzanne's again as she had mouldy fruit and never washed her neck?'

Existentialism proves hard to keep up at home.

I roll my eyes and she helps me locate the tent. Once again, I have the twitch of guilt, but brush it aside.

We take the Friday off school and meet up with Bob the Van, staggering under the weight of essential items for a three day music festival. Lip gloss features heavily in the luggage, as does nine changes of clothing each, plus five different sorts of shampoo. We are laden down with make-up remover, spot concealer and Aqua Manda body lotions. We have no toilet paper and, *not* surprisingly, I am the only one who has brought any food along (a massive lump of cheddar cheese, pinched from the fridge, pots of yoghurt that we can't do without and a fruit cake that Strawy made for some tea time gathering that I deem an unnecessary extravagance and would be far better suited to the drug fuelled food cravings of three stoned teenagers. I reason it thus: I am doing something so awful, that the mere fact of pinching a lovingly made cake is as nothing. Nice, huh?).

Bob the van's friend, Marty, insists on sitting in the back of the van with us. He is already so off his face that he can barely talk, let alone navigate, which is, apparently his forte. He has packets of pills falling out of his pockets, that he intends selling and a carefully nurtured stubble. His long black curly hair is shining with conditioner but if you can ignore that, and his mockney accent, he is a nicely brought up boy from the middle classes and reasonably fanciable.

We set off to catch the ferry to the Isle of Wight. We don't actually know where the ferry sets sail from but this is a minor problem. We are confident that we'll find it. We are after all on a holy mission, surely the vibes of Jimi the guitar god will safely guide us to the designated place of the miracle? Bob heads vaguely towards the sea. This seems about right.

After a trying conversation where we can't decide if the Isle of Wight is really the Isle of Man we stop to buy a map. We haven't got enough money so Michaela shoplifts it.

'All property is theft,' she tells us, triumphantly holding up the map *and* a bag of apples while waving cheerfully at the poor shopkeeper. We eat the cheese and fruitcake in the van, reserving the yoghurt for emergencies. We can barely see one another in the back of the van, the smoke of joints is so dense. Marty is mostly comatose.

The van breaks down very little, considering it's mainly held together with rust, wire and fervent Jimi expectations.

On the ferry we experience our first taste of freedom. I get a jolt through the spine when I realise that *no one* at home knows where I am.

The Isle of Wight resembles a war zone. The freaks and the yippies are at war with the anti-capitalists who want the festival to be free. They in turn can't agree with the Marxists who want to make the vegetarians make peace with the anti-fascists who are arguing with the anti-racists about the validity of the gender divide of the public loos with the women's libbers. Or something like that. The hippies are all too stoned to move very much.

Eventually we get in.

We take about three hours to put the tent up – not helped by Marty who is under the impression that we are trying to take it *down*. The lunatics really have taken over the asylum. I nervously glance around me, and remind myself that this is where I want to be. Don't I? I tell myself that I am having *fun* and that all other feelings are due to paranoia caused by excessive amounts of dope (not guilt).

As far as the eye can see, there are our fellow brothers and sisters basking under the cold grey English sky. I pull Grace Helen's velvet opera coat closer together. I can't actually button it up, because it was made for the days when corsets clinched the waist in to seventeen inches but it looks cool. We set off to the loos, and thence to step over acres of pale supine bodies by the stage.

The horrors of open sewers masquerading as loos on holidays Abroad are nothing compared to a music festival. We mourn the stupidity of crates of hair product but no loo paper. The shampoo etc is useless as there is no hot water on the entire island. Marty trails behind us, gurning horribly.

Free are playing, and our stomachs churn in excitement. Rumour has it that John Lennon has just arrived by helicopter and there are over 500,000 of us. The air is so thick with dope smoke that we shouldn't really have to roll a joint for days. Night falls and things hot up. We have made lots of new best chums, the sort Strawy would definitely not approve of. Michaela has had five 'encounters' with really cool men. Suzanne and I stick close together and try not to let the side down by not looking cool. The Who come on and we all frantically dance with strangers who become friends for an hour or so. This is the life, we tell ourselves, passing and accepting joints from the crowd. Marty is falling over a lot while a very attractive white foam gathers in the corner of his mouth. Ten Years After come on. We are in seventh heaven. Jimi is due on soon. We decide to repair to the tent to beautify ourselves for him. After all, it is just possible he may spot us in the dark amongst half a million mad people.

Suzanne obviously has better directional skills than me as she finds the tent with only a minimum detour of an ever spiralling two miles. The overwhelming smell of cheap hot dogs fills the air and I know with certainty that, however hungry I am, I will never eat. They are unnaturally pink. The alternative is the hippie stands selling macrobiotic brown rice with the occasional fish head thrown in for luck. Yuck. It strikes me that I am a food snob.

I am starting to feel anxious. What if Strawy calls Suzanne's mother? I confide my worries to Suzanne, who I can tell has been thinking along the same lines. She isn't as affected as I am with the worry that maybe Strawy has found out and I am not where I said I would be.

We comfort ourselves that Jimi will be on soon and all will be well. Marty lurches into the tent and falls over. His pupils are so dilated that he looks demented. His legs are flailing wildly around in an attempt to catch up with his arms. He looks like a fly dancing on its back. We try to straighten him out by offering him an apple. He starts to weep at our kindness and declares eternal love for us, and as proof of his devotion he *gives* us a couple of pills.

We eye them doubtfully.

We don't want to ask what they are, as that would definitely be uncool. On the other hand, I am not about to chuck something unknown down my throat. I glance at Suzanne and she, with the attitude of a hardened opium eater, casually asks what they are.

'Mandies,' is the baffling reply.

We look at one another blankly. 'Won't she mind?' we ask naively.

Marty elaborates. 'Mandrax. They're fucking *great.*'

That's enough for us and we swallow them with a gulp from the outsize bottle of cider that Bob has stashed in the corner of the tent.

We pile as much make up on as possible and discuss what Jimi is probably feeling right now. I have a flash of unreality as it hits me that I am about to see my god. His is the only poster I have on my wall, his is the only LP that I air guitar to in private. I love him. I want his babies. I tell Suzanne that I think he won't be feeling nervous as he can feel the love.

She tells me that she thinks he is the re-incarnation of Krishna.

We clutch at each other in rapture at the thought that we are soon going to be so close to him that we'll almost be able to *see* him. We re-apply our make up and brush our hair. Again. We finish the cider and discuss the pros and cons of being married to Jimi. How we'd cope with the fame and the groupies. Obviously we couldn't tie him down, he'd have to be free to be the creative genius that he so clearly is but we'd make sure that we went everywhere with him. Even to the bathroom, probably. We carefully apply a glitter butterfly transfer to our foreheads, and douse ourselves again in Aqua Manda.

As we unzip the tent fully ready to sacrifice ourselves on the fire of his genius. We slowly, gracefully slip to the ground, fast asleep.

We wake the following morning, fully dressed with our make up plastered to our faces so tightly that I can't open my eyes and for a moment I am convinced I've gone blind.

We have *slept* through Jimi Hendrix's performance.

The enormity of this takes a while to sink in. How could this have happened? I turn accusingly towards Marty but he is nowhere to be seen. I am speechless with rage. Suzanne just cries. Tiny Tim is on stage and he's crap. I want to go home. Now.

The weekend drags on and it soon becomes clear that

Bob, Marty, *and* Michaela have gone missing in action. Suzanne and I abandon the tent, get on the ferry and hitch home, fortifying ourselves with cider and joints. Just outside Southampton, a kindly middle aged couple give us our coach fare home. I think they believe we won't make it otherwise. They could well be right. Suzanne is still crying and I am so hungry that I feel sick. I am very stoned, and more than slightly drunk. We hold hands on the coach, muttering death threats for Marty.

Some sort of maternal jungle drums have got through to our mothers who are waiting at the coach station.

Strawy's blue cold look convinces me I will never be allowed out again. Suzanne's mother, on the other hand, is very, *very* verbal. She is still shouting as Strawy grimly closes the car door on me and drives home.

I timidly ask how she found out.

She snorts with derision and drives furiously home, shooting through a red light and narrowly missing a cat on the road.

Back home it's even worse. Uncle John is clutching a forbidden glass of whisky and shoots me a look of such anger that I bolt upstairs, locking myself in the bathroom. I take advantage of such existential delights as hot running water and soak in a bath, not before glancing in the mirror and seeing that I am liberally covered in mud and still have a faded yet unmistakable butterfly clinging to my brow.

I venture downstairs to face the music.

The truth is, I am, of course, delighted to be home. The Isle of Wight was messy, dirty, and more than a bit scary. I am beset with anxiety and guilt and I am *starving*.

Strawy is banging things around in the kitchen and it is left to Uncle John to point out the glaring awfulness of my behaviour. I take it on the chin, rather handsomely, I think, and apologise profusely. He gives me a cuddle and asks if Vera Lynn was performing. I punch him playfully on the arm and dare to go into the kitchen.

My mother is making me snape and grilled bacon. I greedily eat a plateful and sidle up to her for a cuddle. We spend a long time hugging and toasting crumpets in front of the fire that is specially lit for me. I make a solemn promise that I will never, ever do such a thing again.

Have I got away with it?

No, not really.

I am forbidden to go out for a month and Suzanne and I are not allowed to see each other out of school. Far worse than all of that is that Strawy no longer trusts me. Quite right too.

This was the beginning of the end between my mother and me for a couple of years. I was out of control. She was out of her mind with worry. I started dealing acid at grammar school and was packed off to boarding school. Suzanne went to art college and Michaela went to live in a commune in Hastings.

I learnt that I wasn't cut out for a life of wild rock and roll – not enough comfort for me. I like to know not only where the next meal is, but what it's going to be. Smelly loos, no food and communal living were what I yearned after but home was where my heart really lay. Well, where my stomach was.

Chapter 11

Remember, We're English

Moules

There is a world of difference between eating a bad mussel and being allergic to them – so don't worry.

Wash and beard the mussels under cold running water. Chuck any that are cracked, open or at all damaged.

Melt a little butter in a large pan, and sweat one or two chopped shallots and a clove of garlic.

Add the mussels and a glass of white wine. Slam the lid on the saucepan, and shake gently for about four minutes. The mussels are cooked when they are opened. Throw in a handful of chopped parsley and eat with good bread.

My mother decides that we are going to drive to France during the long boarding school holidays. We will spend a night or so in Paris with friends then head out to the coast somewhere. We will take along a few chums.

This *sounds* OK but Strawy has never taken a driving test. She was driving long before they were mandatory and was just randomly issued with one. A *grave* mistake. She has her speeding tickets and written cautions framed and hung in the kitchen. She is very impetuous by nature and never more so than when behind a wheel.

Fortunately we are taking along Naz, a mild mannered friend who is in the middle of a nasty divorce but *likes* driving, and Lizzie, my Uncle John's girlfriend.

My mother and I have become best friends again, to our mutual delight. My wild years of being a grumpy socially inept adolescent are *practically* over and she and I have agreed a truce. She makes me laugh more than any other person I have ever known, and I bathe securely in her love. This doesn't stop me, quite rightly, from being very concerned when in a car with her.

Uncle John is in America on business but when he calls I tell him about the driving holiday that we have planned and he tells me to take a first aid box and to wear my seatbelt at all times, even if we are just parked by the side of the road with the engine turned off.

We are all going to stay with Jaqui and Guy, and their daughter Kati, who is my age. They are great friends and I have stayed with them on and off for years. They live in an elegant villa in Le Vesinet, a suburb of Paris near Versailles. It's where I learn to make the perfect vinaigrette. We call and tell them when to expect us.

We pack the car up, and head off. Naz starts to weep the moment we leave the driveway, sobbing that his wife has destroyed him. He is a poet, and my mother tells him that his work will improve with a broken heart and a change of scenery. This makes him choke and Lizzie helpfully hits him on the back, somehow cracking one of the bones in her little finger on what she later describes as his 'bloody hard poetical ribs'.

We stop off at a chemist where her hand is taped up.

Naz confides in us that he has contemplated suicide once or twice and my mother tells him that he might as well sit up in the front with her then as that might be an easy option if he isn't feeling brave enough to do the deed himself. Naz snorts appreciatively and settles down.

On the ferry, while trying on sunglasses in the duty free shop, I spot Naz's wife, Julia, with a tall handsome man. They are clearly besotted and I whisper my discovery to Lizzie and Strawy. We decide to buy Naz lunch in the restaurant to keep him away from her.

Four courses later, we are all groaning with food. The ferry is French and the food delicious but the quantity perhaps unwise for a channel crossing: mouth watering moules, bloody steak, stinky cheese and sticky fruit. We are also knocking back rather a lot of wine. Naz is happily unaware that Julia is on the boat and proposes a stroll around the deck to work off some of the lunch.

'Nonsense,' my mother says firmly, 'Four brandies, please.'

An hour later we are docking in Dieppe and Naz is looking rather green around the gills. Strawy puts this down to excessive food and drink and the rocking of the boat. But I see that he is clammy, with sweat trickling down his face, and prophesy that he is going to be very ill indeed.

By this time we are all sitting in the car, in the dark bowels of the boat, breathing in petrol fumes and admiring the insouciance of the French sailors, waiting to get off. I spot Julia and the handsome man in a car beside us and, to distract Naz, I offer him a mint. As he reaches to take one, he spots them.

He goes berserk. There really is no other word for it.

He flails around trying to open the car door. We are vainly trying to hold him back but he gets shouting that he's 'going to kill the bitch!'. Wrenching open their car door he starts to drag Julia out so he can reach across to the man and batter him with a duty free bottle of brandy. The normally gentle Naz is screaming and shouting profanities we never knew he knew. Just as he reaches his climax of rage he stops and does two things at once: vomits violently and passes out.

By now, all the cars around us have emptied themselves of passengers, trying to get a better view of what all the fuss is about.

The French sailors, spotting a good drama, have held up the queue of cars from disembarking and gather round offering incomprehensible advice. Julia is shrieking and wailing. Her companion seems stunned. One of the sailors points out that Naz seems to have stopped breathing.

'*Il ne va pas,*' he says in pantomime French to us, shrugging at the obvious stupidity of the English.

Julia wails even more loudly and various want-to-be heroes, who may or may not have recently completed a first aid course, offer contradictory advice. No one seems that keen to actually do anything which could well be due to the pools of vomit now surrounding Naz.

'What has he eaten?' Julia demands, pulling at her hair and wringing her hands.

I recite our lunch to her.

'Mussels? Oh my god, he's allergic!'

At this point, a striking looking sailor, that I have been eyeing hopefully, leaps forward, wipes Naz's face and gives him mouth to mouth while thumping his heart area at regular intervals. We all stare horrified at the spectacle.

'Why did he eat them, if he knows he's allergic to them?' I ask.

'Perhaps the death wish was real after all,' Strawy whispers diabolically.

The sailor continues to breathe into Naz while we hold Julia away from him as she seems determined to hamper the procedure by trying to fling herself over him, weeping and wailing. 'Oh, Naz darling, I am so sorry! How could I do this to you? I love you darling! Please, please forgive me!' and so on. Ad nauseam.

The French sailors reluctantly go back to work with a lot of Gallic shrugging, leaving us grouped alone in the rapidly emptying boat. A doctor is summonsed from the port and we all stand around feeling helpless, watching the strenuous efforts of the sailor still breathing life into Naz.

The handsome companion, after taking one last look at Julia who is now hysterical, drives off in a cloud of exhaust fumes.

A French ambulance arrives and relieves the sailor of his duties. Naz looks *dreadful*.

How can a simple little bivalve wreak so much havoc? It seems impossible. I, of course, start to feel that I too may well be allergic to them. My mother assures me I am most definitely not and accuses me of drinking more than my fair share of wine at lunch.

'Though,' she points out happily, 'Grace Helen had an allergy to oysters and they say that it is genetically inherited.'

I try to subdue the queasiness I feel by sucking mints.

We repeatedly thank the sailor for his efforts and clamber back into the car with Julia to follow the ambulance.

Julia is weeping uncontrollably and I ask hopefully if I am allowed to slap her. I've seen this done in the movies, usually to hysterical women. Now seems the ideal situation to try it out.

'I don't see why not,' my mother replies, waving her thanks at the sailors who guide us down the ramp from the ferry. We hit the bottom rather harder than anticipated and lurch around.

The confusion in the hospital is enormous. We can't find Naz's passport and, to make matters worse, there is the language barrier. My mother speaks French like Winston Churchill, making absolutely no allowance for accent or grammar, whilst mine, which seems fine out shopping with Kati, is not up to medical questions. Lizzie is too busy to help as she has taken charge of Julia who really seems on the verge of being committed to some sort of French institution for the rest of her life.

After hours of this nightmare, we are allowed eventually to see Naz. He is propped up in bed wearing a seraphic smile. I suspect drugs are involved in this expression and I am right. He is loaded.

'Total body shut down. I think I may well have died. I feel *fantastic*,' he proudly informs us.

Julia hurls herself at him and we retreat, leaving them snogging on the narrow hospital bed. The doctors show us an x-ray of Naz. It seems he has several cracked ribs. We are not sure if this is due to Lizzie's vigorous back thumping or the efforts of the French sailor who undoubtedly saved his life.

We decide to leave Julia with him and progress thoughtfully to Paris. Because of Lizzie's hand, she *can't* drive, I *don't* drive and we've lost Naz to the post-mussel ministrations of the hospital and his wife. This leaves my mother in charge of a car heading towards Paris in the early evening, after a large and liquid lunch.

Lizzie and I eye each other nervously and hang on for dear life. Strawy races with any other car and anyone foolish enough to slow her down gets a sharp toot of the horn while she mutters 'Out the way father!' Neither Lizzie or I have the heart to caution Strawy, who looks twenty years younger and is clearly revelling in the speed and freedom this drive is giving her.

Poplar trees flash by, leaving us with a sort of French epilepsy caused by the narrow flickering of the setting sun between the trees à la strobe lighting. As we hit Paris, it is dark and the rush hour is full of men rushing at breakneck speed to get to their mistress's before returning to the *petite femme*. Strawy is determined that no driver shall get the better of her but, despite her efforts, we are bested by an enormous roundabout. We all gradually realise that we are being forced into the inside lane and simply cannot break free or turn off. Giant lorries making the evening run to deliver wine and cheese to a grateful populace make this even more frightening. My mother is having the time of her life.

'*On y va!* Out of my way you Froggy brute!' she happily cries out of the window, whilst taking the roundabout for the third time.

It's like being stuck in an outer circle of hell. The

roundabout is truly gigantic, far worse than Hyde Park corner, and thick with French traffic that pays no heed to any signalling, or it seems traffic lights. They seem to think they are merely a suggestion, not a command.

The sixth swoop round we all start to feel nauseous and my mother makes a supreme effort to *get off.* We scrape the side of a deux chevaux and make apologetic faces as the driver shakes a fist at us. We brake hard behind a Renault and bump them. But eventually escape making a smart turn up a one way street where French drivers and pedestrians shout at us. We finally arrive at Jaqui and Guy's four hours late.

After a lot of fractured French explanation and handshaking and kissing we are propelled inside. A group of smartly dressed *tres chic* people, drinks in hand, stand to greet us. They are groomed to within an inch of their lives, showing up our state of dishevelment in a humiliating manner. A dinner party, we are told, to welcome our English friends. My heart sinks. I have experienced these dinners. They are delicious, but endless, and after the day we've had, all I really want is a glass of water and bed. We all look and feel sweaty, dirty and frazzled. We make ineffectual dabs at our faces and hair which render no noticeable result but make us feel slightly better.

We are rushed to the table, and soon sitting in front of us is a colossal, steaming bowl of mussels.

I gulp.

Lizzie, with a great deal of quick thinking, makes a sympathy bid, holding up her bandaged hand and pleading for just a small piece of bread to toy with whilst the rest of us enjoy our moules. She gives me a narrow eyed glance of triumph and then winks.

I glance at Strawy who is sitting beside me. I am not comforted by what I see. She has that determined thrust to her chin and the look of rising to a challenge in her eyes. She takes my bowl and hers and fills them to the brim.

I glance doubtfully at them, remembering poor Naz.

'Remember,' she hisses *sotto voce* at me, 'We're English after all!'

Chastened, I duly nosh.

The cry of 'We're English after all!' covers many emergencies, food and non-food. Handed a plate of dry seed cake by an elderly aunt? Munch away, bearing in mind that we are English. Presented with a plate piled high with leathery beef and sinew at a posh lunch party in Rome? Remember, we're English. Feeling slightly sick? No matter. We're English and we can bloody well eat anything that any damn foreigner cares to serve us.

There are, of course, limits. Years later I am in a tent in the outskirts of Morocco producing a TV series. I had been made an honorary man for the night (thank god, only for the night, I mutter squatting on the ground). I am handed the ubiquitous glass of tooth achingly sweet mint tea and then allowed the choicest cut of meat: a fatty lump of lamb's tail briefly frazzled over a fire. I can feel the director's eyes bore into me as I stare in horror. He is desperate to film this group of people and we are at the end of a long day of heavy negotiation. Eating this lump of dreadfulness was important. 'We're English,' I thought as I forced it in my mouth and tried to swallow. My throat closed up. I gamely battled on, struggling against gagging. Defeated, I pretended to swallow then deftly removed it from my mouth and dropped it into the waiting maw of my handbag. The director was gagging on the second choicest cut. We may be English but we women have our limits.

Chapter 12

A Horse Walks Into a Bar and Asks for a Whisky...

Fish Pie

I lb of cod
I lb smoked, undyed haddock
(or any other fish that you like the look of)
bay leaf
1/2 pint of prawns
2 hard boiled eggs
1 1/2 pints of parsley sauce
(with a good dollop of Dijon mustard)
sufficient creamy mashed potato to cover

Place the cod and haddock in the parsley sauce and simmer gently. The fish will cook very quickly and don't forget it's all going in the oven anyway. Peel and cook the potatoes. Add the prawns and chopped eggs to the fish and sauce and pour into an ovenproof dish. Cover with mash and bake in an oven till brown. Then make sure you invite me over to supper.

For ages now I have been waiting to feel like an adult. It

never really happens. I leave boarding school with remarkably few qualifications and mooch around at home for a while. Strawy pleads with me to think about going to university but I won't.

I take a series of extremely odd jobs to while away the time until my true vocation calls. I stare longingly when friends tell me that they are studying to be a vet or are training to be a lawyer. How do they *know* that this is their life work? What happened? Were they sitting in the bath one day when a bolt from the blue shot them out of the hot water, clutching a flannel to their brow and crying, 'Yes! Of *course. That's* what I must do! I shall spend the rest of my life with my hand up a cow!' I wait for a similar epiphany. None occurs.

Some of my jobs stretch the credulity of John and Strawy to the point of hysteria. Gift wrapping in Harrods – a total disaster when I am handed a circular silver cocktail tray that is wider than the roll of gift paper. I try my hand at waitressing with similar results – 'what do you mean you've been waiting for an hour? Of course I've put your order in, oh, whoops, it's still in my apron!' As a book shop assistant I am convinced I am better suited to *reading* all the new arrivals than selling any of them. As receptionist at a very grand architects I distinguish myself on my first day by pushing through the shredder a long awaited cheque for half a million pounds. I sort eggs, make and sell cakes and have a go at working in a Turkish Bath. Most of these jobs last a matter of days, not weeks, showing what I like to think of as *flexibility*. In those heady days if you left one job at midday you could be in another by tea time, filing your nails.

Then, it happens.

I find myself in a place where I feel at home and where seemingly anything can happen. It's exciting, dynamic, cool, trendy and, above all pays, obscenely well. What is this amazing job? It's almost the Eighties. Where do you think? Advertising of course.

Our main meeting of the day concerns where we're going to have lunch. And whose account it's going on. The agency in question – even now, I cannot tell you the name of it, let's just call it JDV, and if there *is* an agency called that it wasn't them, if you see what I mean – was at the height of its ruling over the consumer world. We had every cool and groovy account there was to be had. A leading jeans company paid for us to sit on a beach in Spain brain storming its new campaign. Cue lots of sangria drinking and very little creative thinking beyond the genius idea of putting gorgeous young nearly naked male models in said jeans and oiling them up. It's a dirty job, but someone's gotta do it. I actually had that put on a tee shirt.

I am the assistant to the assistant art director. And if I don't like it I can always ask *my* assistant to do it. I soon have the delights of my *own* office. I am promoted horribly quickly and have the uneasy feeling that I am about to be *found out* for impersonating an actual adult. I spend a lot of time looking over my shoulder repressing the urge to point at myself and say, 'Who? Me?!' when asked anything in meetings.

Our offices are a vast plate glass nightmare. Men in roller-skates whiz up and down corridors. The uniformly skinny receptionists wear tiny black dresses and red lipstick and have scowls and Sobranie cigarettes dangling from their

117

mouths. They peer out behind large glass vases of lilies. They all have headsets with little microphones attached and spend their entire time connecting the incoming calls with ruthless inefficiency. They continue personal conversations with practised ease.

'Hello, JDV ... one moment, I think he's in a conference call with New York. I'll put you on hold. Anyway, I said that I didn't want to go to the Embassy, and he said that he'd cook at home, Is he mad? Who eats at home now? Who *eats*? I know I can't. I want to try colonic irrigation ... Hello, JDV ... no she's on a shoot, due back next week. Anyway, we had some charlie and the next thing I knew ... Hello, JDV ... what do you mean you want to make a complaint about an ad you saw last night on TV? Get a life ... So there I was ready and willing, and you'll never guessed who walked in ... Hello, JDV ... no she's at the studio. Leave a message? Well, you *could* I suppose ... Yes, only his bloody wife! I mean to say! Hello, JDV...'

This is heaven. Nobody seems to do anything much at all but they do it with style. The main thing is to *look* like you're frantically busy. People carry filofaxes the size of Victorian family bibles so they can see if they have a window for coffee. You see them stop in corridors and consult their page of the day ... nah, can't make three, what about half past? Great, I'll pencil you in.'

I work for Jake. He is Welsh. He is considered the Michelangelo of all the agencies. He is a large man with a greying ponytail and has a weakness for truly terrible shirts. He drives a Ferrari, has a wife in Swansea, a cottage in France, an apartment in New York and a girlfriend in Paris.

He introduces me to the three hour working lunch. We *reel* back to the office in time to return a few phone calls before deciding which wine bar we'll go to that evening.

I seem to spend a lot of time in wine bars.

They are a new phenomenon. Wine bars are the new pubs. Pubs are the old caffs. Wine bars sell food. Of a sort. Some good, some bad. It all depends on how many bottles of champagne you've had. But it all has one thing in common, It is very, very expensive and you can pretty well guarantee that it will come garnished with kiwi fruit.

We also go to a few private members' clubs in Soho.

'Hi, what do you do?'

'Oh, nothing much.'

'Which agency?'

Chez les Anges is pretty and smart and full of media types whiling away the hours till they have to go and do something. It still is only now it's called the Groucho. Jake knows exactly how much he can get away with, always pulling his man of genius card at exactly the right time. His expense sheets alone are a creative work of fiction. We manufacture receipts and then stomp all over them to make them look used. Taxis are used all the time for everything. Need to do a bit of shopping? Get a cab and get a receipt, JDV will pay. Need to go to the hairdressers? Same thing. We treat JDV as our personal bank only it doesn't issue overdraft warnings. Jake has furnished all of his houses and taken most of his holidays on his expense account. I quickly pick up the bad habit and Strawy gets a new gas cooker and a greenhouse. Everyone else does it too. I am surprised JDV can pay the *rent* let alone our stupid salaries.

119

We are presented one day with a new account. A biggie. One worth a lot of money to JDV. It is for a certain brand of whisky. We're not that impressed though, no telly advertising, just below the line posters and magazines. We'll think about it later, we tell ourselves. The weeks go past and the memo about the new account drifts down inexorably in the piles of paper stacked up in our In Tray. Well, it would be an In Tray if we had one. What we have instead is a mountain of paper. I haven't seen anybody add anything to it but day by day it grows seemingly organically. We call it the slagheap. It leans against the wall and is about five foot high. Jake decorates it with fairy lights at Christmas.

We troop off to *Chex les Anges* for inspiration and lunch. Calves liver in green peppercorn sauce and a bottle of house white. We are *working*, after all. We wave to a few other agency loafers and settle down to lunch. We order another bottle. A few friends join us. The manager asks if we'd like to try a new wine he's brought over from Australia. We snigger, but give it a go. New World wine? Chardonnay from *Australia*? It'll never catch on. Several bottles later we spy a receptionist from JDV waving wildly to us from the doorway.

This is unheard of. Certain animals are never seen out of their habitat. It's deeply worrying. You're more likely to see an elephant stomp down Oxford Street than one of these scarlet lipped harpies out of the office.

'Johnnie Deveraux is waiting for you,' she hisses.

We blanch. Johnnie Deveraux is the D in JDV. He *never* comes in. I don't remember the last time I saw him. I don't think I've *ever* seen him. I've heard about him, we all have, he's a legend in all our lunchtimes.

120

'What does he want?' Jake asks, gulping down the dregs of his wine.

'The meeting, you know the whisky thing . . . the client's with him.'

We look blankly at one another.

'I gave you the brief, it's on your slagheap,' The harpy hisses.

'Shit.'

The client is someone we all strive never to meet. We leave that to the suits. We are the *creatives*. Not the bloody accountants. The memo about the whisky account must be buried deep within the slagheap. Even if I raced to the office it would take me a day to find it. I reach for my wine and, seeing that my glass is empty, I reach for the bottle. That's empty too. I stare at Jake seeking reassurance. After all, he's the boss, isn't he? Everything's going to be all right, isn't it? What I see brings very little comfort. Jake is staring glassy eyed and whey faced at the table. I can tell he's pissed, as well as pissed off. Well, so am I. So are all of us. It's lunch time for Chrissake.

'Jake, what are we going to do?' I ask frantically.

'Sssh, I'm thinking.'

I order black coffee and sign for the meal. The receptionist has stalked off, telling us that she will tell Johnnie that we are *on our way*.

Jake is muttering to himself, and I restrain the cowardly urge to walk out of the club and go home. This is serious. The bloody *client* is there after all. We are due in a meeting to present something that we haven't got a clue about. Rising hysteria grips us. The coffee burns our mouths but we gulp it down. Jake glances at me.

'Put some lipstick on, brush your hair and smile a lot. What do you drink with whisky?'

'I don't.'

'What?'

'I don't drink whisky.'

'But if you did?'

'Well, I suppose, American, on the rocks, with—'

'That's enough to start with. OK, ready?'

I nod and we set off to the agency. We are slightly unsteady on our feet but fear has sobered us up wonderfully. Jake is muttering to himself and asks how much a really great looking grey horse is to hire.

'I dunno. I'll find out, What are you thinking about?'

'What do you see if I say American?'

'Umm, well, what about one of those amazing basketball players, or a cowboy I suppose, or—'

'Enough.'

I shut up and offer Jake a mint. We are still sucking them in an effort not to blast the client and Johnny off their seats with our wine breath when we burst into the conference room. I am sober, but have very sweaty hands. The room is full of people. The Clients. *And* Johnnie Deveraux with several henchmen and women looking very tight lipped. I hiccup, and try to turn it into a cough.

Jake is *brilliant*. He doesn't apologise for being late, or for the lack of storyboards. He launches straight into the attack.

'Branding is what this is all about. Whisky is dead. We've got to make it cool again. This is how we're going to do it. We are going to make them ask for *your* whisky,' he points dramatically to the client, and pauses theatrically, 'by *name!*' He goes on to elaborate a series of ads. All starring a beautiful white horse, as photographed by the *best* photographer in the world in the *best* locations in the world. The campaign will be beautiful, witty and win awards. More importantly, it will *work*.

The client is impressed. Johnnie is impressed. Even I am impressed. Johnnie shoots me a look and opens his mouth to speak. Oh god, I just know he's going to ask me a question, one that I obviously won't know the answer to. He taps his fingers on a sheaf of papers in front of him, and says ominously. 'So, Laura, indulge me. Break down the budget on this shoot for me. How much is the horse for instance?'

'A grand a day.' I say firmly, looking him straight in the eyes. I bless Grace Helen for teaching me poker.

A smile spreads over his face. 'We can cope with that. Plus expenses or all in?'

I've learnt enough from Jake to know that *nothing* comes without expenses.

'Plus,' I say, stifling another hiccup.

We get out of there as soon as we can and lurch back to our offices. Jake starts to make phone calls and sketch pictures simultaneously. I have a thumping headache but Jake looks triumphant. I am shocked at the dawning revelation that he really cares about all of this. His reputation is secure. I phone Strawy and ask her if she knows anyone with a beautiful white horse who would like to loan it to us for a thousand pounds a day.

'Oh we'll find one darling, don't worry. I'm in the middle

of making fish pie so ask Jake if he wants supper tonight.'

We take a taxi (natch) home and devour the food. Jake is more than a little in love with Strawy, I can tell. He tells her that if he were thirty years older he'd make an honest woman out of her. She snorts with derisive laughter.

'Not if your behind was hung with diamonds my boy!'

Sitting at home with the delicious fish pie and sobering glasses of water, the world of advertising seems an awfully long meaningless way away. It makes me realise that although today was exciting, I am not cut out for the world of JDV. I lack the requisite qualities: ruthlessness, ambition and the belief that advertising is really, *really* important (even when you're busy pretending it's pretentious crap). I worry, needlessly, that my nice line in bullshit will be wasted in another profession.

The ad campaign was a huge success. The grey horse that Strawy found was plastered over every billboard and magazine in London. It was my job to paint it white. Jake picked up some sort of award in the shape of a golden sphere that he gallantly gave to me who gave it to Strawy. She used it as a paperweight for a long time and eventually it became a prop for one of the pantomimes she wrote and produced every year. I last saw it in a production of Aladdin as one of Widow Twanky's ornaments. Jake would have liked that.

Quite without warning and certainly without prior advertisement, Darling Uncle John dies. I am touched that Jake and loads of others from JDV turn up for his funeral. They even pay their own taxi fare as a mark of respect, though I suspect the massive arrangement of flowers and crate of champagne went on expenses. God bless JDV.

Strawy's fish pie becomes a constant. It grounds me completely and is the antidote to excessive fancy food or just fancy. It's the best advert for comfort food I can think of.

Chapter 13

In Love and In Italy

Sauce Vierge

(or Divine Green Virgin Sauce. Really, really good with practically anything)

> *1 large bunch of flat leaved parsley*
> *couple of garlic cloves*
> *couple of anchovy fillets*
> *tbsp of capers*
> *tbsp gherkins*
> *Slug of good olive oil*

Whiz all the ingredients up in a blender till smooth. This will keep in a glass jar in the fridge for at least a week. I doubt you can keep from eating it for that long.

I take a three month contract job as a photographic stylist in Florence. A good friend, David, is out there and listens sympathetically as I moan about how much I hate advertising.

'Come and work for me. You'll love it,' he says, knowing my weakness for all things Italian.

I take very little persuading.

Strawy, who has nightmarish memories of her entire luggage being stolen in Naples as two policemen smilingly looked on, begs me to take a money belt that I can wear *under* my clothes. I poo poo the idea and catch a plane to Pisa where David is due to meet me at the airport. The flight has a very surreal feel being, as it is, chock full of Italian nuns. They make me nervous. I mean, we've all seen those films. There's always a single nun on board if your plane is going to crash. I've got a whole flock. I look nervously around for a sick child because they always get saved. If I find one, I'm going to sit next to it. The impossibly good looking Italian air crew are very deferential towards the smiling nuns treating them to glasses of Chianti which they refuse and I swig down unchecked. Even the food on Al Italia is divine: tiny rolls stuffed with prosciutto and basil. By the time we land in Pisa I am stuffed and tipsy.

David is faithfully waiting for me at the airport but with the gloomy news that there is a train strike and we'll have to get a bus. The happy nuns join us as they too are destined for *Firenze*.

David wants to know if I have brought him Marmite and his dinner jacket. I assure him that I have. I ask him where I am going to stay, pleading that I can't live for three months in a model flat again as I did in Milan.

'Nah, don't worry, I've got you a room at Gilbert's —' David pronounces it *Jillbearr*, which makes it sound a lot sexier than Gilbert.

'Who?'

'Gilbert's. He's another photographer, French, I think. Anyway, you're staying there and I'm next door but I'll have to move in with you next week because Kathy with the feet is coming back and I really think that I might have to kill her and then I owe money to Stefan, so it's all very tricky but we start work on Monday. There's a dinner party tonight, quite posh, so I need the jacket.'

The bus lurches forward trapping a girl and her suitcase in its doors. The nuns shout a warning to the driver, who ignores them. The girl escapes and watches in horror as her case disgorges itself onto the road. Shoes, underwear and toiletries tumble into the path of oncoming traffic. David, sensing the conquest of a damsel in distress, gallantly offers to retrieve them. This holds the bus up for half an hour as he dodges in between hooting, snarling traffic, triumphantly waving a pair of La Perla knickers above his head. The bus is operatically vocal in its admiration, and the nuns burst into applause. David takes a bow, after taking the grateful girl's phone number, and I don't have to remind myself that I am in *Italy* after all.

Gilbert's apartment is the top floor of an ancient building opposite the Uffizi that we reach through massive oak studded doors opening onto a central court yard. We reach the top by climbing swooping sets of stairs that spiral around and around and around. When we pantingly reach the top it's complete with a minstrel gallery and *servants*. Dinner has been set out on the balcony, with candles glowing on the white linen and tiny jugs of wild flowers gracing every setting. I am in love already and that's even before I meet Gilbert.

He is every English girl's idea of foreign gorgeous.

I sit next to him and behave very badly throughout the

meal. I am so flustered by his presence that I can barely eat – a sure sign that something is wrong with me. He has a battered sort of charm about him. His heavy lazy eyes do more than undress me – they practically take me over the risotto. He reminds me of a beaten up Mercedes: lots of class but rough around the edges. Yum.

When he suggests we pair off after the meal to fly-post Florence with posters for his new exhibition, I knock over my wine glass in my eagerness to go. Soon we are on the warm streets of Florence, armed with a roll of posters. I wave goodbye to David and link my arm through Gilbert's, stumbling over the cobbled streets. We head off down a dark alley and I cling to him squealing as I stagger around. He gently pushes me against a wall and slowly, agonisingly slowly, kisses me. He tastes of garlic, wine and Gauloises. It is the breath of a god. He laughs and suggests, in his broken English, that we quickly put up some posters and retire back to the apartment.

Oh yes please. *Prego*.

The first poster goes on top of a wall of tattered paper. It seems that all the posters from the past ten years are there so we add ours to the palimpsest. As we smooth it on we're blinded by headlights and two carabinieri jump from their car, shouting at us.

Gilbert starts to shout back while I cower behind him wishing I could do more than order a coffee in Italian. Lots of hands are being waved about and the raised voices could well be discussing football results for all I know. It seems that fly posting is illegal and we must pay a fine. OK, I mutter, just pay them and let's get back to the apartment. Pronto.

It's not that simple.

Gilbert has no money on him, I only have English pounds and the police seem bent on making an arrest. Are they mad? For sticking up a poster? Oh god, I have visions of being thrown into an Italian prison, rotting away while David queues at the British embassy. The police are adamant. They have to arrest us. Gilbert tries to explain that he has money back at the apartment if they would accompany us there he could give it to them. But no, with much regretful shrugging, they escort us to the back of their car.

When Gilbert explains to them that it is my first night in Florence they kindly drive us around the city pointing out places of interest with great civic pride. I try to be polite but have more pressing things on my mind. And pressing on my legs. Can we be arrested for making out in the back of a police car? Or, as we are already arrested, perhaps we'll get another fine?

We arrive at the jail, which is reassuringly modern looking and not rat infested. We are offered coffee while some paperwork is completed. The tiny white cups are spotless and the coffee very strong and good. It comes with a tiny almond biscuit which I nibble on whilst taking stock. I wonder if the police would be so obliging in Islington? Stumping up with tea and a digestive?

The police regretfully inform us that while we wait for some money they must, by law, lock us up.

I am escorted to a cell that already contains three hissing and spitting prostitutes in fur coats and wigs. They are utterly terrifying. I sit in the corner, holding my tiny coffee cup of espresso, wondering if I could possibly use the cup as a weapon? And if so, will it go against me in the great fly posting trial?

Gilbert calls to me from his cell, around the corner, that I am not to worry. He also starts a rapid conversation in Italian with the three girls (I use the term loosely) in my cell and soon they are smiling at me. They explain in pantomime Italian that they are not really women, but transsexuals – somehow, don't ask me why, this is quite comforting. One of them, Gina, a six foot six giant with cocoa coloured skin and a Tina Turner wig, is trying to explain the operation to me (apparently the most painful part is having his Adam's apple shaved off). Suddenly David is in front of the cell.

He is very, very cross with me.

'One night. One sodding night and you're in jail. I don't believe it. I've paid the fine, which let me tell you is *massive* as they think we're rich, what a joke that is . . . Stefan's going to kill me as I *promised* him that money. . . Come on Bonnie, let's collect Clyde and get out of here.'

Gina and the girls kiss me goodbye. Gilbert promises to pay David back and we leave the police station but only after the police have assured me that they wish every happiness in my stay in their, 'ow you say, historic and beautiful city'.

It is very late now and we have to walk back to the apartment which is miles away as we can't find a taxi anywhere. The cobbled streets don't seem quite so romantic now, and my feet are killing me. I keep pleading for David and Gilbert to slow down as I am having trouble keeping up in my high heels. We pass a shady looking back street bar and go in for a reviving drink. Grappa all round. Gilbert squeezes my leg under the table and apologises profusely for our unscheduled trip to the police cells.

Back at the apartment David says goodnight, muttering that I am not to get into any more trouble and promising he will pick me up for work tomorrow.

Gilbert slowly smiles at me and holds out his arms. I, of course, rush into them, and soon we're tearing off clothes. I wonder briefly about the wisdom of doing it in the salon of the apartment – what about the servants? But what the hell, this is the dolce vita. I am soon naked and he (who I've had time to notice does not wear any underwear, which is something I'm sure Strawy would not approve of) is the same. We are standing, flesh to flesh, tongues down throats, when I hear the unmistakeable sound of the door being opened.

A woman in a squashy blond fur coat stands there surrounded by Fendi bags. She gasps and Gilbert swings his head round.

I have no need of an interpreter. I know enough Italian and French to understand that Gilbert is a bastard son of a bitch and is – 'ow you say – going to be killed'. I hop around trying to find my dignity and my clothes while dodging the Fendi bags being hurled by Gilbert's exceedingly angry wife.

Gilbert, hopping on one leg trying to put his trousers on, unbelievably makes introductions.

'My wife, Mara, this is Laura.'

Mara halts magnificently, one arm poised aloft with a lethal looking handbag, and inclines her head towards me. She then continues her assault on Gilbert. She soon runs out of missiles and leaps out onto the balcony where coffee cups and wine glasses are the only things left on the dining table. But not for long. All are hurled around the room with devastating aim. I duck the splintering shards and manage to scoot out of the room. I am minus my bra and one shoe. I collect my bag and lug it down the endless stairs that hug the well of the courtyard. The lights, which are on a timer, periodically plunge me into darkness and I am left fumbling blindly for the next switch before running wildly down to the next one. I struggle with the massive oak doors and am finally outside.

Now what?

It's about three in the morning. I have no idea where David lives. He *said* next door but this part of Florence is a maze of ancient apartment blocks and no lights seem to be on anywhere. My Italian isn't up to waking people and asking for an Englishman called David. I start to feel very sorry for myself indeed. I quite like the feeling and give myself up to it. I sit on my suitcase and light a cigarette. Perhaps I cut a romantic tragic figure, like one of those heroines from a black and white foreign movie? I try for a muffled sob but it comes out as a strangled snort. It does, however, attract the attention of a cat that winds itself round my ankles. I absentmindedly stroke its bony shanks, while thinking furiously of the dastardly Gilbert. Enough minutes have passed from the 'No Sex Please, We're British' romp I've just been through for me to start feeling deeply embarrassed. Oh god, not only have I been in jail, I've been caught naked with a near stranger by said near stranger's wife.

I finally stand up and, dragging my case along with me, decide to head somewhere. I don't really know where but I can't sit on the pavement for six hours waiting for David. A hotel, that's where I'll head. *If* I can find one, *if* it's open and *if* I've got enough money. Oh god. I have a sharp urge, that I resist, to call Strawy.

I set off towards what looks like a busy street. Only when I get closer do I realise it is indeed a busy street but it's full of girls who look remarkably like the one I said goodbye to in the prison cell.

I am in the notorious street of transvestite/transsexual hookers. Oh *great*. They all take an instant dislike to me resuming their hissing and spitting. What *is it* with these guy-girls? Do they think I am about to move in on their pitch? Highly unlikely, giving that I am at least twelve inches shorter than any of them, *not* wearing a wig and, surely this will settle the matter for once and for all – despite my tawdry episode with Gilbert, am *not* a hooker?

I see the lights of a coffee shop and, braving the cat calls and hissing, stumble inside. My arm feels as though it's about to drop off but I really can't take any more of the hissing. The owner of the bar looks surprised to see me, as well he might, considering the other clientele. I can tell he's surprised because the ash from his fag drops into his coffee and he keeps drinking it and keeps watching me. The whole bar feels menacing. I start to regret coming in.

With a show of bravado I do not feel I ask for a coffee.

He doesn't acknowledge he's heard me but continues staring at me. I can feel hot prickles of sweat break through my armpits, as I envisage Strawy waving her finger at me warning me about waking up as a sex slave. If this was going to happen anywhere, this place is it. Perhaps he'll slip something on my coffee and I'll end up in a back street of Naples not knowing my name?

To my utter delight, I see Gina sashaying into the bar still wearing her Tina Turner wig. I fall on her like a long lost friend and she hugs me. The atmosphere lightens somewhat.

I tell her my story, and she orders me breakfast, waving away the proffered money.

'All men are bastards,' she confides, leaning forward to adjust her cleavage.

A plate of *something* arrives, and she gestures for me to eat.

I stare at the plate, not wishing to hurt Gina's feelings and gingerly cut off a small corner of the frilly white square of the thing that is quivering there. I can no longer resist knowing what it is.

'Burger. Florence burger.' Gina gestures proudly towards the plate.

Huh?

I catch a whiff and, looking down again, I realise it is, in fact, tripe. This delicacy comes with a dab of iridescent green sauce on a tiny saucer that I am meant to dip in. I'm too scared not to but I wish I hadn't. The sauce is divine. The tripe is not.

I glance around and see that this is the working girls breakfast. In Naples they have *pasta puttanesca* (literally tart's spaghetti). Named so, because it only takes the girls a few minutes to knock up between clients. Here, in Florence, they have tripe. Oh lucky, *lucky* me.

I was eventually re-united with David and we spent three months photographing shoes and handbags with skinny models in the Boboli Gardens. Gina became a good friend and we exchanged Christmas cards up until recently when she died back in her home town of Sao Paulo. She requested to be buried in her best wig and scarlet sequined dress. I hear they had quite a party. I think of her every time I make the sauce vierge.

I love making food that reminds me of friends. As I chop the parsley the smell instantly takes me back to the hot summer in Florence when Gina was in between clients and could take a moment to eat with me. Her cage of songbirds would be twittering on the dusty ledge of her minute window through which the sounds and smells of the city squeezed. She taught me how to make sauce vierge, how to mix the perfect martini, how to remove any stains from marble, how to make gnocchi and the ultimate tomato sauce.

David and I would often visit her and sit knee to knee on her bed as she rapidly cooked something on her one ring cooker. I can still hear our laughter. Her wigs were scattered over the floor, like the scalps of her many conquests and we'd carefully step over them. After we'd eaten we'd go and have an elderflower sorbet, sitting in the sun. She advised me *always* to check if men were married. And do you know? I always do. I never assume a woman is all she strives to appear to be, too.

Gilbert's exhibition was a success but Mara caught him with the gallery owner's daughter and took him back to Paris. I never saw him again. Thank god.

Chapter 14

Emmets

Cornish Pasty

These bear no resemblance to the shop bought ones at all. This is not a classic recipe but one that Odessa used to make for high days and holidays.

Pastry – easy peasey
1 lb plain flour
1/2 lb of butter
pinch of salt
water

Rub the fat into the flour, add the salt and then add the water gradually until it comes together without being too sticky. Set aside in a cool place.

1 lb lamb
1 large potato
1 onion
large bunch parsley
salt and pepper
half pint of cream

Cut the meat and vegetables into small pieces but do not mince. Roll out the pastry and, using a small plate, cut out into circles. Moisten the edge with milk and support half of the pastry round nearest to you with the rolling pin. On the other half, put some of the meat and vegetables. Season. Sprinkle a dusting of flour over the filling. Fold the other half of the pastry over the filling and squeeze the half circle edges together firmly. Now you are ready to crimp the edges together, leaving a small hole in the centre. Brush with egg wash.

Bake in a hot oven for twenty minutes then reduce heat and bake for a further forty minutes.

Chop the parsley and stir into the cream. Whilst the pasty is still hot, carefully pour a little of the cream mixture into the small hole on the top.

Eat with both hands and a napkin to catch the crumbs and the juices, my lover.

Strawy buys a haunted house in Cornwall to open as a B&B. St Anne's has a leaky roof, a secret passage leading to a priest hole, a hidden well and a friendly ghost that smells of pipe tobacco.

I am delighted for her but miss her dreadfully.

The wild gardens have a paddock with a salmon river running through, a run down pig sty and a bamboo grove. Camomile grows wild between the rocks. It is enchantingly run down.

Rabbits and squirrels nibble on Strawy's seedlings and she takes careful aim with a shotgun. I *say* careful – the aim is to frighten, not kill. She takes up salmon fishing and has great success with a bamboo rod and a lump of smelly Stilton, much to the amused delight of the anglers who come here.

Cornwall is a strange, heady mixture of poverty and eccentricity which suits her well. The nearest neighbour is, undoubtedly, a witch. She has the unlikely name of Odessa. She lives in a tiny cottage up the lane and knows everything there is to know about plants and healing. She has a medicinal herb garden that would put any physic garden to shame. She is spherical and has lived in her cottage all her life. She goes into Bodmin about three times a year and has never left Cornwall. She can tell the sex of unborn babies, forecast rain and read tea leaves. She teaches Strawy how to make clotted cream, keep bees, and make sloe gin. She quizzes us about London with a mixture of pity and curiosity.

'Reckons it's fearful crowded and dirty, innit, my lover?' She really does say 'my lover'.

We assure her it is, and that she's not missing anything.

'Still, wouldn't mind seein' that flower show they'm have in Chelsea. Seen it on the telly, looks a right proper job.' Odessa adds wistfully.

Strawy arranges it as a surprise and they set off together on a coach, leaving me to hold the fort at St Anne's. They are to be gone for two nights.

St Anne's has no neighbours, other than Odessa and she is gone. There is a water mill about half a mile away and a pub a mile up the hill. So I'm glad that the house is full of fishermen, whose only demand is a large, cooked breakfast at the ungodly hour of six thirty so they can be on the still misty banks of the calm river by seven.

141

This means that I have to get up at five. This seems so unlikely that I consider staying up all night so I don't oversleep.

The aga sits spreading warmth in the massive kitchen but *only* if you have fed it with foul smelling coke the night before. *And* riddled it. *And* cleaned its dust off it with a goose wing. It all seems like a choking amount of work. I eye the beast doubtfully. Why can't they have cornflakes or something?

Nevertheless, I set the alarm and am staggering around the kitchen at ten past five. Bacon, eggs, mushrooms, tomatoes, hog's pudding and toast. Tea *and* coffee. It takes *forever*.

The fishermen gulp everything down leaving me with a mountain of dirty plates and a feeling that maybe the French really do understand about breakfast after all. I mean, how hard can it be to take delivery of fresh croissants and warm some milk for the *café au lait*?

At ten, I've just finished washing up when I hear an almighty crash from the road going over the hump backed bridge outside. This small bridge spans the river Camel, and is very, very narrow. A massive lorry has jack knifed on it and the driver, who appears to be all right, is standing in the road looking bewildered. I take him inside for tea and let him use the phone.

He's from up country (this can mean anything in Cornwall, from being, god forbid, Welsh, to a Londoner or just from Devon). He's delivering a consignment of shoes from a well known chain of shops to a shop in Truro. He's on the phone for ten minutes or so then goes back outside to his lorry. He comes back, astonished. The lorry is completely empty.

He wearily gets on the phone again, to his boss and the police. I sympathetically make more tea and wonder how it happened. We are miles from anyone, how did the lorry empty itself so quickly?

Eventually the police and an even bigger lorry arrive and the damaged vehicle is towed away. I survey the endless empty cups and start washing up again.

About four there is a knock on the back door and I see Arthur. Arthur is the water bailiff *and* the local poacher. He sometimes leaves peel (young salmon) wrapped in leaves outside the front door or a rabbit, neatly skinned, with a bunch of parsley.

'Afternoon, my lover, now then, what size you'm be?' he says, removing his cap and rubbing his silver hair with the flat of his hand. He has the eyes of an innocent. Pale blue, set in a weather beaten, unlined face. He must be at least seventy and looks as fit as a fiddle. He normally wears gum boots but, as I follow his proud glance downwards, I see that today he has on a pair of very snazzy Italian loafers.

'Now, your mum, she'm be a right little'un, so I reckons she's what, a three? Mebbe a four?' He gestures towards the sack that he's carrying, where at least twenty pairs of shoes are all jumbled together.

I stifle a giggle, and tell Arthur that Strawy is indeed a size three.

He leaves only after I have chosen three pairs for Strawy and a pair for myself. He gravely explains that no money need change hands, as after all, the windfall happened right outside the house, and therefore is really ours anyway.

To satisfy my curiosity I ask how the lorry was emptied so quickly.

He puts one finger to the side of his nose, and winks. Then he's gone.

The following day Strawy's back. I ask her how Odessa liked London, and the Chelsea flower show. My mother groans, and puts her feet up on a chair. I hand her a gin and tonic, and she smiles her thanks at me.

'Well, as soon as we crossed the Tamar and left Cornwall, I think she expected Highwaymen or something and spent the whole journey clutching her bags. When we finally got to London I thought her eyes were going to pop, she'd never seen anything like it. The crowds! The shops! We got to the hotel and I made sure she was OK in her room then I told her I'd pick her up in an hour to take her to dinner. I thought she'd like that little Italian place run by Marco, you know? Anyway, when I went to knock for her, she wasn't there. I searched the hotel bar, reception, everywhere, I couldn't find her. I got very worried – I mean, she's practically an innocent abroad, I had all sorts of things going through my head—' I snort with laughter as I imagine Odessa part of Strawy's kidnapping fantasy.

'Anyway, I finally tracked her down to the hotel kitchen where she was busy showing the chef, a very nice man I must say, Polish, you know, how to make a pasty... We ate in the kitchens that night.'

'But what about the flower show, did she like it?' I ask.

'Like it! We were nearly asked to leave!'

'Why?'

'Because Odessa had nearly every plant that she could

find secreted about her person! Now you know me darling, I'm not averse to the odd cutting now and again – but this, well, honestly, Chelsea would have been laid bare had I not intervened!'

I snigger, and tell her about Arthur.

We conclude that Cornwall is still a county of wreckers – the ancestors who lured cargo-laden boats onto fierce rocks are alive and well in Arthur and Odessa.

As I leave to go back to London I see that Strawy is wearing a new pair of pale pink suede shoes with a very attractive kitten heel.

The county of Cornwall is still one of the poorest places in Great Britain. What economy there is, is based on the emmets (ants) of tourism. Fishing has declined and the tin and clay industry is dead but the romance lives on. It is a magical place and I firmly believe King Arthur is still there somewhere. It is the foodie's region and, as regional food makes a certain kind of comeback, it will profit: the freshest fish, heavy thunder and lightning cream teas and the sticky saffron cakes the Phoenician traders brought with them and traded for precious tin are all in the county.

When Strawy first moved to Cornwall grilled mackerel and salad was 30p in the Fisherman's Arms in Padstow. It's now about £8.50. But just as nice.

Chapter 15

Dinner Parties from Hell...

Good Tempered lamb

This truly is one of those dishes you can forget all about, it's so forgiving.

Leg of lamb
Garlic
Lemons
Salt
Olive oil
Fresh Rosemary (lots)

Rub the lamb with salt. Make gashes in it and insert the garlic, squeeze the lemon over it, then the olive oil. Make a nest of the rosemary and place lamb on it in the roasting tray.

Roast till it's done how you like it. Pink or falling off the bone, it's always good.

It's the early Eighties and we all give dinner parties. Strawy is in Cornwall and I am married, living in London. The husband in question runs a small graphic design company (hey, who doesn't?). Our dinner guests are clients. Sometimes they are fun, sometimes they are *not*.

Tonight's couple is an unknown quantity. Paul and Carol may or may *not* be giving us a contract. I set off towards the shops in a great hurry as my apricot standard (that means *very* large in dog terminology) poodle, Folly, is about to give birth and I don't want to miss it. I beg a leg of lamb from the butcher who also gives me a massive knuckle bone he has saved for Folly (a great favourite with him as she often pretends I have stepped on her paw outside his shop and howls till he comes out with a delicacy for her). I pick up some lemons and artichokes from the greengrocers and hurry home. Pudding? I'll find something in the fridge or make do with fruit and something.

I let myself in and find Folly wedged against the cooker, whimpering. I call the vet (for about the tenth time that week and he assures me all is well. All right for *him* to say, I think looking anxiously at my dog, what would *he* know?). I stroke her and she pushes her head into my leg craving attention. I spend an hour sitting on the flight of steps that lead down to the garden with her, drinking tea, and trying to encourage birth pains. She's been due for ages now and I am getting worried.

I trail inside and she follows me pantingly to my desk where I settle down, supposedly for an afternoon of work. This never really happens. If you have ever worked from home, you'll know. People *know* you are there and, even if you explain as to a small child, that you really *are* working and, as much as you'd love that cup of tea/glass of wine/gossip about the boss/let the washing machine repair man in/lend the black dress, you can't, because you are *working*. All my friends are impervious to my bleated protests now and march through the door, heading straight for the kitchen and the fridge. Even husband seems to have no respect for the sanctity of my job (the job I moan about all the time ... writing copy for a video company is hardly curing cancer but...). He calls all the time asking daft questions. *Has Folly had her puppies yet?* (Duh, I would have called *you*.) *Is there any chance of you ever making my favourite dinner sometime in the next year or so?* (No. It involves boiling sausages in baked beans – learn to make it yourself.) *Could I just pop to the dry cleaners and pick up a suit that I have to have for tonight? And is it OK if my brother and his girlfriend spend the summer in our spare room?* (Yes to that question, as his brother is *divine* and I am trying to convince myself that I have not married the wrong brother, which over time proves to be the case, but that's another story.)

I have to contend with all of this, plus a call from my boss who has had a fraught train journey from Scotland and wants me to find out where Lord Beeching is buried so that he can piss on his grave. (As I recall it's somewhere in Derbyshire, and said boss went there with a few bottles of lager and duly did the foul deed.)

Time flies by and I am engrossed in a fascinating conversation with gay best friend about the beastliness of Sir Georg Sholti (GBF is a fiddler at Covent Garden and it seems that Sir Georg had the temerity to suggest that the orchestra would like to rehearse the national anthem on their *own time*) when I hear a piteous cry from Folly. I follow the sounds into the kitchen where she is, undoubtedly, *at last*, about to produce puppies.

I call husband immediately pleading with him to return

home. I then ring the vet who I am told is out on a call. I give Folly some warm milk with sugar in it as instructed by all the dog books I've read then impulsively add a slug of brandy. Folly laps it up then howls and moans for a while. The sound is heartbreaking and I am in a state of nervous panic by the time husband finally gets home. He takes one look at our (I use the word loosely, because, frankly the dog is *mine,* as she knows very well which side her bread is buttered and would die through lack of exercise and food if it wasn't for me) beloved pet. He blanches.

'Oh god, she looks terrible, call the vet again and *do* something.'

I pass him the bottle of brandy and call the vet. *Again.*

Next door neighbour, Maggie, arrives to join in the panic. Maggie is an elderly Welsh diva who used to sing with Dorothy Squires (don't worry – anyone under 50 won't have heard of her and I think she was probably more famous for having married Roger Moore than anything else although she did once hire the Albert Hall for a performance and it sold out). Maggie is very theatrical and is usually on some form of prescribed medication for imaginary illnesses. This week it's some sort of nervous tension that manifests itself in being unable to stay still. She paces the flat, wearing a floaty long chiffon dress with spirals of colours on it that trails over the floor, catching up all the dog hairs. Her long white hair is caught up at the back with a jewelled pin and she sports full theatre make up. She is a *sweetie* but she does dress as though a bomb has exploded in a fancy dress shop.

A messy and loud and worrying hour or so later, Folly

has six enchanting bundles of pale brown fur. She is not cut out for motherhood and takes very little interest in them beyond a cursory lick. We, on the other hand are behaving like cartoon parents. If I had a cigar I'd light one. I notice that the bottle of brandy has gone down and phone Strawy with delight to tell her the news. Maggie demands to speak to her and I hear them cooing over our bundles.

'Oh darling, they are gorgeous! And I win the bet, it's three bitches and three dogs! So you owe me a tenner. Do you really want Laura to keep a bitch for you?'

Maggie hands me the phone and I reassure Strawy that she can have a puppy. Strawy asks me what I am going to have for dinner. Dinner! The possible new clients! The lamb should have been in the oven over an hour ago and the kitchen-office and dining table-desk are more than a mess. It looks like a dog maternity ward/bar. I put the artichokes on, shove some garlic and lemon in with the lamb and go to throw it in the oven. As I do so, I nearly step on one of the puppies which has wriggled away from Folly. In trying to avoid it, I side step and drop the lamb on the floor, which is pounced on by Folly who, as she stands up, with a neat suction sound drops all the puppies who were feeding from her.

Maggie rescues the lamb from Folly, who quite rightly feels her ordeal entitles her to some red meat. The doorbell rings and husband admits Paul and Carol.

It's not good.

He is wearing a suit and tie, *she* is wearing a knee length cocktail dress with a sequined animal motif on the left breast, they are clutching wine and flowers.

151

I try to see with their eyes what they are seeing and fail dismally. I am used to Maggie (who now looks like a demented Lady Macbeth, wiping her lamby hands on her by now very messy long flowing number). I am even used to husband (and trust me here, that takes some getting used to. He wears a spectacularly vivid Hawaiian shirt in a sort of 'post modern ironic I am a graphic designer sort of way'). I lower the eccentricity count by wearing black leggings and leg warmers. (Don't you dare say anything, we *all* wore them, it was the Eighties. We *did*. Honestly.)

I perform miracles, simultaneously sweeping the dining table free of clutter, pouring drinks, slapping on some make up, getting changed, making nibbles to stave off hunger pangs (as the lamb is going to be ages) *and* getting Folly settled. All in a matter of minutes. I shoo people into the living room and try to appear calm and efficient and *welcoming*.

Paul and Carol perch on the edge of the sofa looking terrified. Maggie is pacing the room, hair coming adrift while she regales them with the time that she found Tony Hancock naked in her bedroom setting light to the curtains. Husband is pouring drinks with the abandonment of a man who knows that the evening *and* the contract is doomed. We might all just as well get very, very drunk.

I, on the other hand, am determined not to give up so easily. I engage Carol in conversation. She has a small tightly pursed mouth, tiny blue eyes with the bright whiteness of eyeball that proclaims the non-reader, non-drinker, non-entity. She keeps her hand firmly clenched on her husband's arm. Her gaze drifts around the room absorbing the shock of every unpolished surface, the groaning floor to ceiling book shelves, Strawy's unbelievably bad oil paintings and the flowers she has brought still lying in the cellophane. I jump up to find a jug for them and she offers to help me. It's unfortunate that she trips over the knuckle bone that the butcher gave me for Folly but I don't think she hurt herself *too* badly.

By the time we get to the table, we are all quite drunk. The lamb has fairly obvious dog tooth marks in it which I manage to carve around making sure Paul and Carol don't get any. Maggie eats with us, but not actually *at* the table – she wafts around the room clutching a plate to her bosom, dripping lemon and garlic down her dress.

Carol is drunk enough to unbend slightly and she confides that this is her first night out since having her baby.

'How old is it? I mean, *her*. Or *him*, of course!' I say, frantically trying to remember if she has told me before. I feel slightly sorry for her, and try to imagine leaving the puppies for the night.

'Only eleven months,' she says, adding coyly, 'It's a girl, Angela, would you like to see a photograph?'

I nod enthusiastically, while trying to keep control of my elbow which has unaccountably slid off the table. Eleven months? She hasn't been out for eleven *months*? It sounds like a prison sentence. I am appalled, and try to think what it must be like. Is this normal? I mean, once you have a baby, is that it? Do you never go out again? And if you do, you end up somewhere like *this*? I now feel really sorry for Carol and am determined she have a good time. I fill her glass with wine and gesture towards the other bottle. Husband takes the hint and opens two.

Pretty soon Carol is my new best friend and we dance around the room with Maggie. We find another bottle of brandy and Paul asks if we have any of that drug that he's heard about, but never tried, you know, stuff that goes in a *joint*.

Husband and I stare blankly at one another. What planet are these people *from*? We haven't smoked dope for years now but we've probably got a tiny amount lurking in a box somewhere. Husband eventually finds a minute cube of dope in the back of a drawer and obligingly rolls one for Paul and Carol. They titter and behave like very naughty school children coughing and spluttering their way through the joint. Maggie *finally* sits down, exclaiming that she feels quite tired and can probably sleep now. Husband escorts her to next door while Paul and Carol sit picking at the remains of the lamb. They're not quite so fussy now about the tooth marks, I notice. I abandon them to go and check on Folly.

As I am in the kitchen, I reason I might as well do the washing up and start swishing plates in hot soapy water. The puppies really are enchanting and I wonder if I could sneak one upstairs to sleep with me. This is probably not a good idea though Folly looks as though she wouldn't mind. I trail upstairs, flicking lights off and soon am fast asleep. I vaguely hear husband come through the kitchen door (he vaults the garden fence from Maggie's as a short cut). Soon we are fast asleep.

The following morning I find Paul and Carol fast asleep on the living room floor, swathed in a throw from the sofa and a goat skin rug.

I am *mortified*.

I stumble apologies, but nothing really covers up the fact that I had completely forgotten them. So had husband, although he insists he assumed they had gone because I was in bed.

Paul assures us he has had the time of his life. Carol begs me for the lamb recipe. And we get the contract.

Chapter 16

Eating With Hands

Roasted Asparagus

Ease and luxury all combined…

> *1 large bunch of English asparagus*
> *Splash good olive oil*
> *Sea salt*
> *Black pepper*
> *Balsamic vinegar*

Set the oven to high. Very high. Trim asparagus by holding up one stem at a time and snapping it. It will naturally break where it needs to and you will be able to eat the whole thing. Place on roasting pan and drizzle with olive oil, sprinkle with salt and pepper. Shake pan till all the asparagus is coated, turn oven down to high/medium and pop in till faintly singed. Immediately dash balsamic vinegar over and eat with fingers. Heavenly.

Gay Best Friend, Philip, has met a new man. This is very exciting news. Philip was in despair at never meeting anyone – he's *very* exacting. Some would say pernickety to the point of impossibility. But the new man, I am assured is *perfect*.

Philip wants Strawy and me to meet him. He suggests dinner then has an even more daring plan: a weekend away, just the four of us.

I am horrified. I don't think it's the sort of thing that should happen at *all*. Why would the new man want to be saddled with us? Doesn't Philip want to take him somewhere romantic *à deux*?

Philip sounds guarded, in fact he sounds slightly shifty.

'The thing is, well, he's very, well, umm, *cultured*, I suppose is the word that I'm looking for and he has this hobby, well, I say hobby but really, it's more of an *obsession*, I think, and I thought that if there were some other people about –'

I demand instantly to know what the obsession is. I am already imagining terrible things, like Victorian pornography or enemas or dolls. And if the new man is so bloody cultured, what does he want with us? Because Philip is a violinist, I consider him the most cultured person I know. He even listens to that awful modern stuff, you know, the sort of music that's described as *challenging*, and actually likes it. *And* he can quote Shakespeare – no, not just all the old chestnuts, but stuff I've never heard of. Strawy and I use him as our walking dictionary and quotation book. What can we bring to this party for two?

'Well, the thing is that I'd feel a lot more comfortable with you both there, you know? Please . . .'

And the obsession? I demand

It turns out that the new man, William, is rather obsessed with churches. Not so scary.

Strawy is, as ever, delighted to swan off for the weekend, even to Chichester and the unknown quantity of a B&B. We duly throw a few things in a bag and wait for Philip to pick us up. The car draws up and we jostle one another at the window to get a first glimpse of the New Man.

'My God,' Strawy hisses at me, 'He looks like Lytton Strachey!'

I take a peep. She is absolutely right.

Philip has the glow of pride of all new lovers as he introduces us. William is so tall and so polite that even though the introductions are done in the car he uncoils himself and gravely shakes our hands. He is wearing a very rumpled linen suit, a dubious hat and has a long, bushy beard. He is very, very thin.

We set off for Chichester with Philip behind the wheel, frantically making conversation. We try our best to keep up but I can see that we are letting the side down, as the talk is mainly of orchestras (of which the tone-deaf Strawy and I know nothing) and churches (ditto).

William has a curiously high voice and makes little snuffling noises in lieu of laughter. Strawy nudges me hard with her elbow every time he does this and I get the giggles. We stop for tea en route and attract a few curious glances. Philip is a small, neat creature which just emphasises the extreme tallness of William. He is also, like a lot of tall men, gangly and hesitant. He looks *exactly* like he would be interested in churches.

Over tea he confides that he has a penchant for brass rubbing, snuffle snuffle, and I feel the elbow coming my way again but avoid it by bending to retrieve a fallen napkin from the floor.

I stare at Philip trying to see William as he does. I fail

dismally and resign myself to a weekend of severely bruised ribs.

We set off again, and eventually, after a few missed turnings, hit our B&B. I note that Philip and William have separate rooms but this could just be the natural reticence of Philip. Strawy drags me into her room, and we giggle uncontrollably at William, the velvet clown paintings on the wall, the *nylon* sheets and the dripping shower.

Wiping our eyes, we saunter downstairs to find Philip glumly waiting for us.

'You hate him, don't you?' he says miserably and I am beset with guilt.

'No, not at all, he's just, well, he's –' I stumble.

'Darling, if you love him, I'm sure we will, we just need time to get to know him, that's all,' Strawy says, kissing Philip on the cheek. I eye my mother and see that she is being absolutely sincere. *Not* for the first time, I wish I had her easy way with people.

William joins us and we head for the cathedral. William walks into two children, a lamppost and a tree during the short walk there and I feel my mouth twitching. He's quite endearing about these bumps, and stops solicitously every time to apologise and snuffle ruefully.

After what seems like *weeks* of gazing appreciatively at stained glass windows and dusty naves, I start to flag and slope off, towards the main doors. I am soon joined by Philip who looks *exhausted*. We agree that the cathedral is wonderful but simply can't spend any more time here. We're cathedraled out.

Strawy and William are still in deep discussion about

something and are pointing things out to each other in the soaring roof of the church.

Philip glances admiringly at them and so do I because I know with certainty that my mother knows absolutely *nothing* about whatever the hell it is that she's pointing out and cares even less. I hear the odd word echoing around the groups of students and tourists from the two of them and I feel nothing but admiration for Strawy's command of ecclesiastical vocabulary.

'How *does* she do it?' Philip asks.

'I have no idea. Shall we go and get a glass of wine or something?' I say, fanning myself with a pamphlet exulting the rare delights of the rood screen.

We set off back to the guest house and are soon huddled over a bottle of white, where I listen to Philip describe how he feels about William.

'Look, I know he looks odd, well, he *is odd*, but . . .'

'It's OK, really, I'm sorry if I'm not overly enthusiastic, it's just that he's not your usual type, is he?'

(The usual type comment was a pretty pathetic attempt on my part to make Philip think he was a man of the world and often brought home chorus boys or something but the truth was that he has never been that sort of gay guy. Philip's partners tended to be shy, fey boys who did things like guitar making, or flute playing. William is just not like that. He is a sharp, brainy man straight from the pages of a Bloomsbury novel.)

'What does he do?' I ask.

'Nothing. Trust fund, I think, although you'd never know it – he lives in a hovel, but has first editions and stained glass collectors call him from Venice. I don't think I'm interesting enough for him...'

'Rubbish. Drink up, where shall we go for dinner?' I say, getting our priorities right.

We ponder this, and then the conversation drifts back to William.

'Perhaps you could get him to cut his beard?' I suggest, unable to imagine how anyone could fall in love with a man who looks as very odd as William undoubtedly does.

'Perhaps ... although even without it he'd still look odd, wouldn't he?' Philip replies.

'But do you care?' I persist.

'Not really, I suppose, I find him enormously attractive with or without the beard, and I do love him, which is such an unusual sensation for me, you have no idea what it's like –'

'Thanks,' I say acidly, pointing to my wedding ring (second one).

Philip rightly ignores this and I hear more that I ever want to about the hidden delights of beardy William. How they met (Philip was playing a mass in a church). How William *never* goes out, unless it's to visit a church. How extremely clever he is, how he *never* drinks, *never* goes to a restaurant.

'He sounds like a bloody saint, or a hermit,' I interrupt crossly.

'But that's the challenge, really,' Philip says complacently. I sigh.

By the time we've finished the bottle my mother and William have still not returned. Wearily we set off back to the cathedral to search for them. The giant doors are firmly closed and, apart from a few stragglers, there is no one in sight.

We return to the B&B but they're not there either.

Philip and I agree to meet one another after having had a shower and a change. I am convinced that the missing couple will be back by then and I go to my room and marvel at the English idea of décor.

An hour later we're still twiddling our thumbs.

'Let's go and eat something, I'm starving,' I say predictably.

Philip looks as though I've wounded him. But I persist. I mean, William and my mother haven't been kidnapped, they are adults and I am *hungry*!

'Come on,' I say, pulling Philip to his feet and guiding him outside. We end up in an Italian restaurant where there are the usual oversized phallic pepper pots and Sorrento murals. After an indifferent bowl of pasta we make our way back to the B&B (actually named Windy Ridge, which of course prompts many schoolboy level jokes from Philip). We spot two unmistakeable figures weaving their way towards us. Well, one of them is weaving, the other, the tiny one, is propping.

We watch in silence as they approach and then run forward to relieve Strawy of the burden that is William.

'Mama, you've got him drunk!' I say accusingly.

Strawy winks at me, and together we haul William up the stairs of Windy Ridge, with Philip wringing his hands at the sight of his beloved under the influence.

I drag my mother into my bedroom and ask where she's been.

'Well, I thought he needed loosening up a tad, and the best thing I know for that, with a *man*, of course, it doesn't work with women, we're all too astute, is to pretend to be *deeply* interested in whatever it is they are and then ply them with wine and make them eat with their fingers. So that's what we did. Simple when you know how darling. Anyway, we had a glorious evening, I quite see why Philip so clearly adores him. You mark my words, now he'll be able to do a church from the outside.'

I marvel at this but keep my mouth firmly shut. I suspect she is wrong but I have seen her proved right so many times I'm not willing to take a chance.

Strawy goes on to reveal exactly what they had to eat – everything she ordered *had* to be eaten with fingers: large garlicky prawns, globe artichokes, mussels, heavenly green asparagus and crusty bread.

We spend a great day in Chichester, don't go to the cathedral again and even pass interesting looking country churches on the way home without William giving so much as twitching. He could indeed now do a church from the outside.

Philip and William have been together for twenty years. William *still* has his beard. After Chichester. William took Strawy to Rome for a weekend where they viewed the exterior delights of the churches by day and sat in trattorias by night licking garlic from their fingers. Philip and I were *not* invited.

Chapter 17

Scars

Thai Crabcakes

4 thin slices fresh white bread
1 small bunch coriander finely chopped
Thumb of fresh ginger, finely grated
1 lime, juice and grated zest
4 spring onions, finely chopped
1 or 2 tbsp Thai chilli paste
2 tsp fish sauce
1 large fresh crab, white and brown meat
1 large free range egg white, lightly beaten
1 tbsp sesame oil

Whizz the bread into crumbs, gently combine all the ingredients together and with wet hands make into cakes. Chill for at least an hour before gently frying in the sesame oil. Serve with fresh lime wedges and a sweet chilli dipping sauce. Delicious.

Anthony Bourdain, in his book Kitchen Confidential, says that all chefs boast about the scars they accumulate over the years. The more scars you have, the more macho you are. I don't know about being macho but I do know that anyone who cooks a lot ends up with a menu written in burns and cuts on fingers and palms, arms and feet.

Strawy had countless burns on the inside of her right wrist because she believed only wimps used oven gloves and that she was somehow made of asbestos.

My friend Ben is missing his little finger, sliced off when he worked as a sous chef in a very busy London restaurant. He was chopping leeks when his attention was caught by Mick Jagger who was using the kitchen as a short cut to the back door to avoid the waiting photographers. Ben's hand was poised with a lethal knife high over the board – he turned his head – and wham. Bye bye little finger. Apparently Mick was most sympathetic and obligingly scrawled his name on Ben's apron in felt pen. Ben says that took a little bit of the pain away – that and gazing at *those* lips.

Another friend, Chiya, was making matzo ball soup for a friend in distress when she slipped on a noodle and broke her toe.

The worst scar I have I blame fairly and squarely on a toffee apple. I was about fifteen at the time and had been tempted by the burnt sugar smell of the toffee apple stall at a school fair that I had been dragged to by Strawy (she was disguised as a gypsy – silk scarf tied around the head, a pair of earrings and a flouncy skirt – as she had volunteered to man the fortune telling tent). I had visions of her foretelling certain white slave trading for all and was sauntering away from the fair to hang around the local record shop with a few fellow disenchanted souls who also found the idea of bat the rat, coconut shies, and sheep herding *far* too exciting

and thrilling to join in with. I was engaged in wriggling off
the last bit of toffee from the apple with my tongue and
probably wasn't paying as much attention as I should have
done to the road. I truly didn't see the car coming.

I woke up in the ambulance, Strawy beside me with a
by-now familiar look on her face.

I lost several teeth, had one hundred and twelve stitches
in my face, fractured my skull and cracked my ribs.

Strawy insisted on a plastic surgeon. The night nurse doing
her rounds found me sobbing in bed, not knowing what had
happened to me or how I now looked. She fetched me her
compact mirror, making me promise I wouldn't tell the
doctor. She solemnly swore that in a year's time, I would
like quite as good as new. I took a deep breath and confronted
the mirror. Frankenstein looked back. My first thought was
– thank god I like reading. I shall never, ever be able to go
out again. It was a horrific sight. Bruised, bloody and swollen,
with a trail of ugly black stitches holding my face together.
I silently handed the mirror back to the nurse and started
to plan the library that I would make Strawy and Uncle
John build for me.

Allowed home the following week, I couldn't get my
jumper over my head, and Strawy had to take off her cardigan
and slip my arms into it. What a comfort it was to be
wrapped in such a familiar scent: cloves, pepper, a hint of
soup and maybe a trace of Madame Rochas.

I spent days in bed – unable to eat anything other than
liquidised bananas, strawberries and ice cream. Everything
hurt so much and was so swollen and bruised it hurt to try
and turn over. But the nurse was quite right. A year later

after another bout of plastic surgery I was OK. All that remains is a slight scar above my upper lip and I could have had that corrected but, trust me, plastic surgery is more painful than reality programmes show and I have grown used to the scar. That was my last toffee apple.

My next biggest scar is on the middle finger of my left hand. I am cooking supper for my flat mate Mark, when he gets a call from his boyfriend. I call out to invite him for supper, eyeing the two salmon fillets I have on the board in front of me, thinking to myself that one of them can easily be sliced in half. I am planning to wrap them in silver foil, add ginger and soya sauce, and bake the parcels. Mark and I retire to the living room with a bottle of wine to wait for Lee. Both boys are trolley dolleys and I love to hear about their near misses, rude passengers, fanciable captains and galley disasters. Apparently, when they run out of tonic water in first class, they add a pinch of liver salts to replicate the bubbles and at very high altitudes they use ear wax to stop champagne from bubbling over glasses. I resolve never to fly first class. If I am ever in that lucky position, I won't actually *drink* anything. Lee arrives with more wine and I slip into the kitchen to prepare supper.

The salmon is slippery and as I pick up the largest fillet to slice it in half a tiny part of my brain that must be endowed with psychic powers whispers to me to be careful. I, of course, ignore it, and, holding the salmon firmly down with my left hand, pick up the knife and begin to slice through the shimmering black blue skin of the king of fish. The knife slips and blood stains the fish. I curse and hold my finger under the cold tap for a while, bodging the rest of the preparation. I wash off the fish and, wrapping a tea towel around my finger, carry on with supper. It's only when I notice the tea towel is soaked through with blood that I wonder if the cut is perhaps deeper than I first thought. Puzzlingly, it doesn't even hurt very much.

I unwrap the towel to have a proper look. I can hear Mark and Lee laughing about something in the living room and Mark calls out to me to ask if he can do anything to help and do I want my glass of wine in the kitchen?

What I see under the tea towel takes a moment or two to register in my brain. I see that the cut starts at the side of my nail and runs downwards for about three inches. There appears to be something *white* in it. What *is* that? Dear god. I am looking at my finger bone. There is something very wrong indeed about this picture, my brain is slowly telling me. Bones should be on the *inside* and definitely not be seen. I feel like someone is holding a cushion over my eyes and then I hear a roaring in my ears. I manage to stagger over to the ever greedy fridge that thrums under my touch and lean back.

Mark and Lee both arrive in the kitchen just in time to catch me from fainting on the floor. I hear the words stitches, and shout – no.

I refuse to go to A&E on a Saturday evening. I am convinced after assiduously watching nearly every episode of ER and Casualty that it will be full of drunks and train crash victims. The boys are *thrilled*. They have, after all, been trained in first aid and know exactly what to do. One of them fetches my wine, whilst the other lights me a cigarette. They then squabble over who is going to apply the butterfly plaster.

Lee wins, after all, it is his first aid kit that he has to bring up from his car. But first they must to staunch the flow of blood. I feel a bit like Tony Hancock in the blood donor sketch, as *pints* seem to have poured out of such a tiny cut. I hear them chant the words – elevate and apply pressure – and they both take it in turns holding my arm above my head and squeezing a new tea towel to the wound. Eventually it stops bleeding, but now it hurts like hell and I demand more wine as a pain killer.

The plaster worked and I didn't need stitches, although they both talked a lot of nonsense about tetanus shots or something that I ignored. I have a raised red scar that runs down that finger now and I wisely get the fishmonger to slice my fish for me.

A few years ago I get a call from David. He has left Italy and wandered around the world, eventually spending his time between Singapore and Thailand. He tells me of the gorgeous apartment he has with polished teak floors, a swimming pool, and the hundreds of tiny, pretty little Thai girls who are all desperately in love with him.

'But can you *talk* to them?' I ask nastily.

He laughs, and invites me out there.

What the hell? I think, and duly book myself a ticket. I feel the need to connect with old friends and am, surprisingly, now old enough to have old friends. The flight is staffed by tiny, pretty smiling Thai girls who offer orchids to everyone on embarking but only seem to answer call buttons if you are a large overweight, ugly western *male*. I pretty much see how the land will lie before I even step off the plane. The heat in Bangkok is exactly like having a hot, wet blanket wrapped around you and I struggle for a sight of David. He is there, leaning on a barrier, as he always is, no matter what part of the world I visit him in.

We take a taxi to his apartment and I am transfixed by the colourful crush of humanity that I see outside the taxi windows. He holds my hand and warns me against another trip to the jail house.

'OK,' I say, chastened.

We hold hands for a bit, and then he starts reading me the riot act about what else *not* to do in Bangkok.

Do *not* touch any animals, especially cats or dogs, as they are all rabid. On no account am I to get a tuk-tuk (those pretty little motorised rickshaw things) as they are *very* dangerous and the drivers are all on drugs. Make ice cubes with *bottled* water. Do not even clean your teeth in the tap water. Eating from food stalls is OK, as long as they are crowded – *never* eat at one that has no customers. Never, ever, *ever* take any drugs *whatsoever* as the police are all corrupt and the sentencing is harsh beyond words. Never pay *anything* without bargaining first. The list is endless and I nod at everything, knowing that it is his way of telling me that he is protecting me and showing his affection for me.

We spend a couple of weeks in Bangkok and then travel around the country for another few weeks. It is the ordinary mixture of *extra*ordinary sights and tastes that make up old Siam. Elephants, sunsets, markets, silks, travellers, horrid old men looking for cheap sex and finding it, beauty, monks and longboats. We make our way back to Bangkok for my final two weeks as David has a shoot going on and I have promised to cook Christmas lunch for the motley group of

Brits, Aussies, Americans and Germans that hang out at David's Blade Runner-like apartment overlooking Lumpini Park & Stadium (where they stage twice weekly boxing bouts I have become addicted to).

I have even got used to the markets and can now haggle with the best of them. What I have not got used to is the teeming throngs of smiling street sellers that cook on the pavement. Woks full of bubbling oil balance precariously on teetering piles while thousands of people jostle past. The traffic is three deep in the roads. Imagine cooking bacon and eggs on the pavement in Oxford street during a heat wave and you will get the general picture.

I have been shopping and am walking home with many flimsy carrier bags full of unidentifiable fruit, vegetables and giant shrimp when the enchanting little girl whose home is above the bar next to David's apartment, but who lives mainly on the pavement, spies me. Her name is Ning, which roughly translates as little mosquito (nice). She has a stock of green coconuts and a rusty machete that she swipes the tops off with. I stop to buy one and, as usual, wince as she hacks away at the tough fruit with the deadly blade. She manages it and proudly pushes a straw in and offers it to me. Burdened down now with the coconut *and* the bags of shopping I stagger off busy negotiating the traffic, a dead rat in the gutter, and all the thousands of people when the inevitable happens. I hear Ning calling to me and I turn around to see her holding up some change for me. I try to gesture that she can keep it but have no hands free to do so. The old woman who is squatting next to her is poking something in a wok and glares at Ning who trips and puts her hand out to catch herself. I drop the shopping and rush to help her seeing with the terrible clarity of slow motion the wok wobble. I get there just in time to snatch Ning and see that the old lady has just missed the handle of the wok. A slick torrent of boiling oil pours from the wok onto the pavement and over my right foot.

Boiling oil. This is medieval pain.

My only consolation is that I am sure I have saved Ning from a terrible accident which she would have suffered from for the rest of her life. At least *I* have travel insurance. Thank god. David appears at the hospital bedside wearing the same look I have seen on Strawy so many times before.

I spend Christmas day in a hospital in Bangkok playing poker with David and eating green coconuts sent in by a very grateful Ning.

Later on, with my foot still swathed in bandages, I hobble to a cookery course run by a smiling rotund Chinese woman in the heart of Chinatown in Bangkok. She proudly tells us that we are going to learn how to make crab cakes. The first thing we have to do, she says, is get our house boy to prepare the crabs. I giggle to myself at the thought of me grandly instructing my flat mate to prepare the crustaceans. She is bewildered by my laughter and even more puzzled when I explain to her that back in England we rarely, if ever, have kitchen staff. Nor do we live with our families.

She looks sad for me. 'You eat *alone?*' she says incredulously.

I nod and I feel sad, too.

Chapter 18

Salt Air

Salad Grace Helen

1 cos lettuce
Handful of watercress or rocket
Handful of young nasturtium leaves
Handful of orange nasturtium flowers
(purely for theatrical effect)

Combine all of the above, tearing the lettuce and savouring the peppery tang of the nasturtium leaves. Sprinkle over some crisply fried lardons, or croutons, or shaved cheese. Dress with a light hand using the perfect vinaigrette to which 2 teaspoons of capers have been added, and a splash of crème fraiche. Fresh, zingy and gorgeous.

If you live near salt water, I am told that you can expect everything you own, even a great big marble fireplace, to erode and eventually break down. This, they say, has something to do with corrosive effect of salt air. My private opinion, backed up by experience, is that it has more to do with the corrosive effect of the five million house guests attracted by the salt air.

I have now lived in a flat perched on the sea front in

Brighton for over fifteen years and can vouch that the salt air does indeed attract visitors regularly, all unerringly stopping at my flat. Most of are very welcome indeed, some not so.

There was that time the gorgeous Christopher came down from London for a summer weekend and stayed with me for eight *months*. He was fun and charming and I still miss him. There was the time that my friend Gillie stayed with me for a week before meeting a young ex-priest and juggler with bright red hair (it's *Brighton*, remind yourself – I still have to), fell in love, got pregnant then narrowly avoided having her baby on my living room floor. She only left after Alice was nearly walking. I am godmother to Alice and bless the fact that her mother met the ex-priest. Then there's the time that Sarah came back from India with a back pack full of spices and stayed long enough to teach me how to cook the perfect vegetable curry. Three weeks. Oh, and how can I forget Nikki, a friend of a friend with nowhere to go, who stayed for a few weeks colonising my spare room, who I finally found wearing *my* clothes and kissing *my* boyfriend? She also took to cutting her hair like mine. Very spooky. It was like having your very own celebrity stalker in your very own living room. I finally got her out by telling her that I was moving to Mexico.

This constant stream of visitors means that I keep a lot of food handy and can hand on heart say I can knock up a meal at midnight for four. Blindfolded.

This really is a gift from Strawy who, throughout my childhood, was constantly in the kitchen making meals for the odd (very odd indeed sometimes) people who dropped in for a night or two and stayed for a year.

I may not be very orderly and organised in other walks of life, the state of my accounts and wardrobe will vouch for that, but my kitchen cupboards are near bloody perfect.

One night I get a call from David who is now living in New York. He demands a list from me.

'A list of what?' I ask curiously.

'You know, life stuff.'

I ponder for a while and realise that he is used to living in Thailand where the girls have shopped for him in the great walk in larder that is Bangkok. David has never really been food shopping. It turns out that he has no food in his apartment whatsoever.

'Buy some pasta, olive oil, mustard, butter, bread, tins of tuna, onions, tomatoes, eggs, bread, salt, pepper, bananas, bacon –'

'Wait, wait, you're going too fast. What *sort* of pasta? How do I cook it? I don't think I can do this...'

David sounds genuinely panicked. I am amazed. This is the man who travels the world with his camera and he doesn't know how to go shopping and look after himself?

The same thing happens when a friend of mine, who must remain nameless (hint: she is a very hard hitting famous journalist and author), proudly calls me to tell me that she has discovered a new way to cook the burgers that she adores.

How? I demand.

'I pop them in the toaster!'

After having explained the dangers of electricity fires and food poisoning I introduce her to the concept of using her grill.

Another friend moves into a flat round the corner from me after a very nasty split with his long term boyfriend. He confesses that he has eaten the same meal every night for three *months*, because he can't cook anything else. (Boiled pasta with a jar of ready made sauce poured over it is not a meal, I say.) This man used to be the head of news at a major TV channel and he literally can't boil an egg.

Other people's food habits intrigue too much for me to leave alone. A friend's boss proudly told her that he had eaten the same lunch for the past forty years (lamb cutlets). Another friend always has the same breakfast: grilled wholemeal toast with a clove of raw garlic crushed onto it, sprinkled with parsley and topped with mung beans and a poached egg for years and years. She says that she hates going on holiday as she knows that she won't be able to satisfy her craving for this particular desire.

One day I am idling away a rainy afternoon doing what I consider the best thing in the world: making a satisfying soup. The phone rings.

'Hi, it's me ... I am at the station, I'll be with you in ten minutes.'

It's Helen. A very good, old mate who has been away doing her high flying job, winging her way around Europe sorting out the problems of large oil companies and their internal security problems. I mean, this woman is a whiz. Truly. She had one of the first brick-like mobile phones.

She arrives looking frazzled and harried bearing horrendous stories of white collar fraud and corporate cover up.

I hand her a bowl of soup and she asks – 'Where did you buy this? I must get some, it's great.'

I tell her that I just made it and she looks at me as if I have just split the atom.

What is it with these people?

I hear people boast about the inability to cook, as if it were something clever. Excuse me? I've never overheard anyone boasting about being unable to have a bath. Or brush their teeth. Or cross the road unassisted. And really, that's how basic cooking is. I mean, I know we don't all have time every day to be Delia or Nigella, but really, get it together. Please.

I don't know what's happening in the kitchens of this country but it's got to be stopped. Now.

I went to a gathering in London last week, a sort of baby shower thing for an American friend of ours, Natalie. Being English, I am not used to them, so I phoned my friend Katie to ask her what I should bring.

'Oh, you know, something horribly cute and expensive from a trendy baby shop,' she said bitterly.

(Katie has been lusting after a baby for some years and despite the fact that she is gorgeous and kind and funny it seems that there are no takers. She is seriously contemplating the two gay men next door and a turkey baster.)

I duly trudge around the shops horrified at the price of cute baby stuff. I'm surprised anyone can afford to give birth these days. Flying in your own Michelin starred chef from Paris every day of the week to whip you up a supper would be cheaper.

The day of the party arrives and, as usual, I am loathe to leave my flat. It is a sparkling spring day, the sort of day that Brighton is *good* at. The beach is dotted with people and the sun is glinting off the waves. It's just the sort of day to put on your sunglasses and saunter along the seafront to an outdoor café and there to wait for one of your friends to arrive because one of them undoubtedly will. *No one works on a day like this.* The dogs have a spring in their step, the pirate like seagulls are swooping down for chips, the gay boys all have new haircuts, the girls have a leg wax and all is well with the world. The gossip about who did what to whom will jump from tea table to table and finally someone will suggest an early evening drink somewhere and we'll all be off. Another day done and dusted in England's hedonistic capital.

But, no. The baby shower is calling. I drag myself to the station and meet Katie. She is wearing the most fantastic hat I have ever seen. It is more confectionary item than headgear and is truly a thing of beauty. Flowers and insects, pearls and mermaids drip from it.

I launch into the old music hall song of 'where did you get that hat?' and she tells me that she bought it instead of a baby present as she was feeling a bit blue. It was in the window of the very posh milliners round the corner from her and she simply couldn't live without it. She's only had it on for half an hour and she's already been chatted up by two divine men. She asks if she can share my present for Natalie and we squeeze room for her to sign the card '. . . and love from Katie'.

I tell her the hat is an investment and I may well invest in one myself. We imagine sloping off from the station and then hitting the promenade to visit all the cafés and bump into all the people we know. We both look one another in the eye, ready to blow out the baby shower, but we can't. We settle on the train where Katie is chatted up *again* and soon are in Natalie's gorgeous Notting Hill flat.

Nat is tall and slim (apart from a tiny bulge which she rubs proudly). She has long tanned, hairless legs and an immaculate pedicure. Her gold cashmere cardi is draped over her toned shoulders. She is beautiful. The flat is beautiful, as are the flowers, the guests, the drinks *and* the boyfriend. It's like being on a set of Homes and Gardens. The wooden floor is spotless, the lighting fantastic, and the presents are all oh so suitable. Tiny sheepskin jackets, baby Elvis outfits, a year's worth of nappies, a pram, a course of ballet lessons and mine (well, *ours* as I remind Katie): a bunch of Day-Glo baby grows with inappropriate slogans on them. I bury them at the bottom of the pile and hope no one notices.

Natalie is so perfect that I am beginning to feel slightly queasy. She throws open the double doors that lead to the dining room and urges us in. She has, she tells us, prepared all the food herself. Since she's been pregnant, she has this kinda earth mother vibe going on. Enjoy! Her boyfriend gazes with awe and pride at this paragon of womanhood that can not only give a mean blow job but cooks as well!

There is an enormous wooden bowl of salad, breads (obviously home made/or bought at the world's most expensive baker in Notting Hill to look home made) pitchers of strawberry and raspberry juice that Katie pours two glasses from (sneaking in a slug of vodka) and fruit. Lots of fruit. Fruit fruit everywhere and not a fruit to eat. Fruit posing on plates. Fruit artfully composed into a pyramid dotted with flower buds. Everything on the table is pink. *For a girl*.

There is a passing nod to kitsch with napkins folded like nappies and stork shaped flower decorations. We all ooh and aah appreciatively and begin to circle the table piling bits and bobs on our plates.

I hurry back to the other room so that I don't get stuck in the African camp chairs and settle instead on a stool which probably is only masquerading as a stool and is in fact probably an ancient Egyptian birthing chair.

I look and look at my salad, trying to guess what it is. When it cannot be avoided any longer I take a bite. It is trout, rhubarb, plums, radicchio, beetroot and peanuts all bound with a redcurrant jelly dressing. I gag. I catch Katie's eye and we get the giggles. I pass on the cake, and swig the spiked strawberry juice, noticing that boyfriend has left all his salad and is no longer looking quite so adoringly at Nat.

Salad covers so many sins.

I go to a wedding, admittedly it is held in a forest, and am served up a salad of white cabbage, pine nuts, mozzarella, bean shoots and brown rice.

A proper salad is not and never should be: 'just take everything you have in the fridge and fling in a bowl slicked with shop-bought mayonnaise'.

After the baby shower and salad soiree Katie and I head home pausing en route for a salad we can actually eat. Katie suggest we buy Nat some cookbooks for her upcoming wedding. I nod, picking trout from between my teeth.

Chapter 19

The Final Cheese Straw

Strawy's Christmas Cake

This is not a fruit cake at all. It's moist and dense and slightly oriental. I always decorate the top of it with a lavish sprinkle of castor sugar, and caramelised lemon slices. Then serve it with crème fraiche. This is a perfect alternative for anyone who finds Christmas pudding just too stodgy.

> 4 clementines
> 2 unwaxed lemons
> 6 free range eggs
> 9 ozs castor sugar
> 14 ozs ground almonds
> 1 tsp baking powder

Simmer the clementines and lemons for an hour or so in water, till they are soft. Drain, and then pulp, making sure you get rid of any pips. Preheat the oven to gas mark 5, and line a cake tin.

Beat the eggs and then add the sugar, almonds and baking powder. Bake for about an hour, or till as done as you like the look of.

Because my life with my mother was inextricably linked with cooking and food, nearly everything I do in the kitchen reminds me of her. I still use her wooden spoon, the handles melded over the decades into the shape of her small confident hands. One of them has a split bowl where she had jokingly thwacked me over the behind with it when we were falling around with laughter at something or other. I can't bring myself to throw it away.

The first Christmas dinner that I cook completely by myself has the effect I've spent my childhood yearning for. It did, in fact, make me feel *grown up*.

Every year, no matter where I was geographically, I returned to Strawy for Christmas. I would join the other hordes on the train and jolt out of Paddington snaking our way to Cornwall. I have even flown to the tiny airport perched on the cliffs with friends on Christmas Eve to find Strawy hopping with excitement (and, of course worry – we could all perish in an air crash before we'd had a chance to taste her mince pies). Mini-buses have been hired and whole house-loads have descended on her, for a week of riotous fun and fabulous food. But however I got there and whoever I brought, I *got* there.

That first year that she was no longer alive felt as though I was the loneliest person on the planet. She died after a supposedly routine operation in September. Grief and horror robbed me of the next few months. Suddenly Christmas stared at me with an icy cold glare.

I loathed the happy shoppers, the TV ads, the piped carols, the smug bloody families. What was I going to do? Where was I going to go? I buried myself in bed, covering my face with Strawy's shawl so that I could inhale the faint scent which was all that I had left of her.

I let the phone ring itself off the hook.

The messages from kind friends that didn't want me to be alone made me even more depressed. Why didn't they understand? If I couldn't have *her*, I certainly didn't want to be part of anyone else's ersatz family.

I realised that I was starting to be clinically depressed. This was something more than mourning, or grief, or anger. A damp black cloud had settled over my soul and I couldn't cope with it. I vaguely wondered about seeing a doctor, but the thought of mewling to him about how unhappy I was filled me with deep embarrassment. Besides, what was he going to do, other than give me happy pills?

I decided that Christmas was cancelled from now on. I made a supreme effort to get *out* of bed and go to the bank. If I had enough money I'd fly off somewhere where they didn't celebrate Christmas and cry for a week or so till it was all over. Then I had visions of some awful sunny beach filled with yet more smug happy families escaping the English winter and curried turkey drumsticks and sad paper decorations put up by the helpful hotel staff for homesick Brits. Good King Wenceslas on steel drums.

That made me so sad I didn't even go to the bank. Besides, just *sitting* on the side of the bed had exhausted me so god knows what actually walking along the road would do. I woke up crying and went to bed crying. The tear ducts in my eyes were sore all the time.

December dragged on and Christmas loomed closer and closer. I began to not only loathe it but to dread and fear it as well. What was happening to me? I gave myself several stern finger waggings. OK, so what was wrong with being by myself at Christmas anyway? I could go and serve food to the homeless, couldn't I? I could hire some videos and buy myself a bottle of champagne and a lobster and not get out of my dressing gown all day. Or, I could, well, you can imagine the desperate list I made up for myself.

I tried to conjure up my mother but she was gone. Gone. It was *lonely*.

I thought about getting a cat. That's when I *knew* I was in trouble. Not that there's anything wrong with cats, I hastily add. But to get one because you can't cope with Christmas doesn't seem quite right. I refused to become a cat woman.

I was dimly aware that by wallowing in my own world of depression I was screwing up a lot of my friends' plans for Christmas. They didn't want to leave me alone but on the other hand . . .

The day before Christmas Eve was probably the worst day of my life. Worse even than Strawy's funeral and I thought nothing could top that. It was grey and cold with a piercing wind and, as I shuffled from the bed to the fridge, I realised with mounting panic that the damn thing was practically empty. So were the cupboards, and the freezer. Worse still, so was the bloody drinks cupboard. I scrounged together some noodles, a tube of tomato puree, ice cubes, frozen peas and a bottle of Curacao.

I couldn't do it.

I couldn't turn into one of those women who live on scraps. I could, technically. But I refused. No I bloody well wasn't. Summoning my remaining courage I left the flat and shopped till I dropped. I bought all the things I should have had and lots of things I didn't need: a great big goose, glossy chestnuts, seasonal fruit, gloriously stinking cheese, tubs of cream and cases of wine all went into the back of a taxi.

'Cor, you've left it late, love,' the taxi driver said, puffing as he helped me unload the goodies from the back, 'Expecting all the family, are you?'

Yesterday this remark would have had me crying and or spitting with rage. To my own surprise, I firmly said – yes, yes I *am* expecting all the family. I raced upstairs and got on the phone.

Robert was surprised and explained that he had got his parents and his sister, *and* her two daughters coming to him and –

'I'm inviting them, too,' I said.

The next call was to Sue. She'd got her grandmother, *and* her brother.

'All of them,' I said firmly.

The strange man in the basement was added (I later discovered he was only strange because he was so cripplingly shy) and all his dining room chairs borrowed.

I think the reason they all complied so meekly was that they could tell that I really *needed* to do this. Perhaps they didn't want to be responsible for sending me over the edge.

The following day I cooked as I had never cooked before. For weeks now I'd lived on snatched sandwiches at odd times of the day and nights, bars of chocolate and the occasional bowl of cereal. The kitchen knives felt foreign in my hand, I dropped an egg on the floor and the sieve flew out of my hands, dusting me with flour. I burst into tears, and sat weeping in my kitchen, the room that had always given me comfort was turning against me. How did this happen? I raged at myself. *How*?

For the first time in my life I cursed being an only child. If I'd had a sister or a brother now they would have eased this terrible rage and grief, surely?

I shakily poured myself a glass of wine. The kitchen was warm with the aroma of the simmering ham and the lemons and clementines cooking slowly ready to be made into Strawy's version of a Christmas cake. I breathed deeply, trying to subdue the tears that I was so sick of.

I allowed myself just to sit and breathe. And slowly, very slowly, I started to feel better. I was doing the things I loved doing for the people that I loved best in the world. Those that were left to me.

I looked down at my hands. They weren't mine any more. Somehow, without my noticing, they had become my mother's. I was wearing her gold ring on my left hand and, as I watched, slowly but surely *she* made the cake. *She* peeled the shallots and *she* chopped the parsley for the stuffing.

From far away I heard her teasing voice, 'What do you say my love, it's cold outside, shall we do what we do best? Time to fart around in the kitchen, I think, don't you?'

Yes. Yes, always. Love and food.

THE END (Nearly)

P.S.

The emptiness I felt on the death of my mother seemed to grow day by day. I remembered the comment by Noel Coward that it was tough to be an orphan at forty. Even that didn't help. The only thing that did help was a never ending series of Midnight Feasts and the grim reality of buying drawstring waisted skirts. You know you're in the grip of a major life event when a cliché hits you with all its original power.

More than the physical longing to see her, hear her, hold her, I craved the connection we had. The shorthand that comes from knowing one other person above all others.

I was adrift in a sea of people that were not my people.

I began to resign myself to never having that bond with another person, and started to question if I was indeed one of those women who having loved once, can never love again. I don't mean men – they come and go in your life. I mean the nitty gritty complex, loving of another person. The shared jokes, the unconditional love, the *knowing* of the other person as if it was one's self.

I was sad and lonely and started to eat to live instead of living to eat.

Then, one day, it happened. Thanks, of course, to a meal. Kung Po Chicken in Soho.

I had gone to the theatre, no, that's wrong, I had been dragged to the theatre by friends. (I don't want to go out, I don't want to meet new people.) On the train we were greeted by a very young, tall man. He was Scottish and enthusiastic and gleaming and just a tad too *peppy* (and gay, although I didn't quite realise at first). He skipped the theatre (wise choice) and turned up for dinner. And he said something to me that made me laugh. Not too unusual, you may think. But I realised I hadn't done it, and meant it, for so long that my facial muscles were stiff from faking polite ha-ha's. I mean, I *laughed*. Really laughed. Rib hurting people-turning-around-in-restaurant laughter.

I invited him for lunch and actually enjoyed cooking for him. He brought me a single sunflower and I served him watercress soup which he fell upon ravenously (like a stray something, he's always hungry and a pleasure to feed). After a bottle or two of wine I roasted a chicken. I wasn't talking about my mother. I didn't need to. It was like having her reincarnated before me: the tiny Strawy in a young Scottish giant. Lunch became dinner became supper and very nearly breakfast.

Months later Damian and I had traded books, had phone cooking (far more intimate than phone sex) and met one another's partners. It was time, we decided, to go away for a weekend. The reason we gave was that we were writing a play together for Radio 4 (which we did). The reality was, we just fancied a couple of days in the country.

The place in question was a haunted vicarage in Somerset, complete with scary dark corners neither of us would venture into and a cooking range that ate logs like a condemned man devouring his last meal. Obliging apple and plum trees grew among the graves in the garden.

While cobbling together an apple and blackberry pie in the kitchen Strawy made an appearance. Not in a ghostly am-dram way.

Music was drifting in from the vaulted main room. Damian had just majestically tossed peelings to the floor (*very* Strawy – she'd clean later) when he swept me in his arms and we executed a foxtrot across the strewn flagstones.

I knew I was home.

He says that I burst into tears. *I* say that I cried becomingly. Either way it worked. I have been home and dry ever since.

Bon Appetit.